W9-DCY-843

DrUGS AND KiDS

Presented to Eastern College by

MRS. & MRS. JESSIE J. SHANK, SR.

in Honor of

FAHAMISHA WATERS

GARY L. SOMDAHL

DrUGS

AND

KiDS

How **Parents** Can Keep Them Apart

WARNER MEMORIAL LIBRARY
EASTERN COLLEGE
ST. DAVIDS, PA. 19087

DIMI PRESS
Salem, Oregon

DIMI PRESS
3820 Oak Hollow Lane, SE
Salem, Oregon 97302-4774
© 1996 by Gary L. Somdahl

ISBN: 0-931625-30-0

All rights reserved. No part of this publication may be reproduced, stored in a retrieval system, or transmitted in any form or by any means without prior written permission of the publisher.

Printed in the United States of America

First Edition, Second Printing

Library of Congress Catalog Card Number: 95-62490

HV 5824 .Y68 S66 1996
Somdahl, Gary L.
Drugs and Kids

Cover design by Bruce DeRoos
Illustrations by Sheila Somerville
Typeface 12 pt. Palatino

DEDICATION

This book is dedicated to my mother and father. They taught me to never lose sight of my dreams. They always directed me to follow my heart and never give up. They showed me how to focus on the future and not on the past. Without the advice and the support they gave me all of my life, this book would not have been possible.

ACKNOWLEDGEMENTS

My knowledge and inspiration in the field of adolescent substance abuse, addiction, and prevention would never have come about without the efforts of others. I owe much to Edward Maloney, MD, the Office for Substance Abuse Information, National Clearinghouse for Alcohol and Drug Information, US Department of Health and Human Services, and the Department of Education. I haven't forgotten the parents and the kids I was fortunate to meet and work with. They were my most unforgettable teachers. And Bill W. for the steps needed to finish what I started.

Many thanks to The Cathedral of the Desert, Dr. Dale White, Pastor Marty Armstrong, and Dr. Stan Johnson. Also, Brenda Harrison, Marissa Straws, Tanisha Straws, Jenna Harris, David Matuszewski, Ron King, Nancy Smith, and Susan Oram. My editor and publisher, Dick Lutz, who believed in me. My son, Geoffrey Patrik Lee Somdahl. And Cathy Shapley who I owe much thanks to for the many hours she spent proofreading this book. Also for the encouragement and inspiration she gave me. She assured me that with patience, come the fulfillment of dreams.

I never will quit thanking my greater power, God. He answered my many prayers.

My dream has always been to educate parents in educating their children about the need to refrain from alcohol and other drugs. This book brings that dream to life.

Gary L. Somdahl

FOREWORD

During my years as an addictionologist, I have read many books concerning drugs and alcohol. I continue to read literature in the addiction field, including books directed toward adolescent problems with drugs and alcohol. I have, at times, been very frustrated with the feeling that while most of these books contained a lot of valuable information, they somehow missed the mark. It was somewhat out of this frustration that a few years back I suggested to Gary Somdahl that he write a book directed towards parents in such a way as to outline in some detail the problem of drugs and alcohol in kids; what parents could do to prevent it, and how they should respond if their own children should be found to be using drugs and alcohol.

It is refreshing to me that Mr. Somdahl's book hits the mark as it concerns useful information for parents. Mr. Somdahl starts off in his introduction by doing a good job of defining the problems of drugs and alcohol in adolescents. He also illustrates how deeply rooted society's denial towards this problem is. It is in human nature to not want to believe that our loved ones and certainly our children, could get involved with these substances but, in fact, they do. It is also quite human to exhibit denial. However, denial which is itself a hallmark of the addiction can be very problematic in that it prevents the proper decisions from being made early in the process of recognition and intervention.

People in the field, of course, see no difference in alcohol or other types of drugs in that alcohol used excessively certainly alters the mind and leads to behavior which is, at best, embarrassing and, at worst, quite destructive. Mr. Somdahl is quite correct in emphasizing to the reader that alcohol is a drug and should not be considered, in terms of its misuse, any different than any other drug.

In Chapter One the author quite nicely details how parents who are adult and have skills that are more mature than their adolescents can be a key player in both prevention and intervention because of these more mature skills.

Chapter Two points out the importance of early intervention as well as the extreme importance of not allowing denial to hinder good judgment. I think this is a theme that threads its way through the book and is probably one of the most important things that parents should remember, that it's quite common to want to deny that this could be happening to their child and that denial can get in the way of proper actions. The case examples that Mr. Somdahl uses are quite good and he has an excellent catalog of signs and symptoms of drug and alcohol use in adolescence.

Chapter Three is an extension of Chapter Two and illustrates how enabling, which often goes hand in hand with denial of the problem, is a very common mistake.

Chapter Three has a very good review of the evaluation process and should be a fine primer for any parent who is preparing to deal with a chemical abuse in their child.

Chapter Four contains some truisms of addiction treatment. It nicely states how getting clean and sober isn't just about not using drugs but is about changing the old habits that potentiate the use of the chemicals.

Chapter Four goes on to deal with denial as well as nicely illustrating the real benefits of recovery. The author does an excellent job in showing that recovery can be a wonderful growth process which could benefit any human.

I see Chapter Five as being a pivotal, and even perhaps, the key chapter in this book. It emphasizes the importance of good family communication and gives some reminders to parents about rearing and enculturation practices that can make for a more stable and, hopefully, a happier home. His comments to adolescents themselves on refusal skills are excellent and often are not included in other books on this subject.

Mr. Somdahl quite properly recognizes the great risk that adolescents are at for suicide in our current society and addresses this very nicely in Chapter Six. Alcohol and drugs certainly compound the risk of suicide in adolescents.

Chapter Seven discusses key points in parenting and parenting skills that can allow the parent to be a key player. The emphasis in this book is on being a key player in the family and in the life of the adolescent child. It focuses on doing this in a very positive and disciplined way which is quite important to cohesiveness in families.

Mr. Somdahl is correct, in my opinion, in stating in his earlier chapters that there have been profound changes in the way our society operates and the effects of these changes on the family structure and the children. I sincerely believe that there is nothing to prevent adults from taking charge once again and structuring families in such a way that they can function more smoothly with greater expression of love and respect.

I worked with Mr. Somdahl as a clinician and observed his clinical efforts with adolescents. He is hard working, sincere, and possesses a unique ability to bond with adolescent patients. I know that he has written a book out of a very strong commitment to strengthening the family structure and decreasing the destruction that drugs and alcohol do in adolescents. My sincerest hope is that parents reading this book will become aware that **all** children in our society are at risk for the destruction that can be brought by drug and alcohol abuse.

Edward H. Maloney, MD

AUTHOR'S PREFACE

Ever since I started working in the field of adolescent chemical dependency, there is one question asked the most of me. Why have I chosen this field of work as my profession? The answer I give is quite simple. It's because I feel obligated to give back what I have received.

Let me be more clear. Growing up in the 60's, the flower child concept descended on me. Feeling the need to go against the grain of conservatism, I chose to grow my hair long, don John Lennon specs, place beads around my neck, and call myself a hippie. Drugs flowed like rivers back then. Seeing the call to become a part of them too, I disregarded all I had been taught about the evils of their use and decided to 'expand my mind.'

As the years flew by like clouds on a windy day, I found myself searching for a peaceful existence. Through constant study of the Koran, the Bhagavad Gita, the Buddha, Kerouac, Cervantes, Gibran, and Casteneda, I still was at war with myself. One day in a moment of clarity, it dawned on me that my attitudes, behaviors, and involvement with mind and mood altering substances was blocking my advancement toward becoming harmonious in heart.

In reading a story one morning about Mother Teresa, whom I consider one of the most compassionate people alive, there was a quote from the Bible. It read:

"Oh divine master, grant that I may not so much seek
    to be consoled, as to console;
to be understood as to understand;
to be loved, as to love;
for it is in giving that we receive;
it is pardoning that we are pardoned;
it is in dying that we are born to eternal life."

It became apparent that if I expected to live a life of peace, happiness, joy, and enthusiasm, I needed to do for others to help them achieve the same. So paradoxically, I feel that I can't keep what I have unless I give it away. It is with this firm belief that I feel the need to work with young lives that have been beaten down by the power of drugs.

The job I have in helping kids who use, misuse, abuse, or are addicted to drugs is, most of the time, rewarding. Especially when they are able to grasp the concept that by living clean and sober lives, they will be able to fulfill their dreams.

And then there is the sad side, too. Often, I have shed tears for those who have chosen to continue on the path of destruction. It's sometimes hard to accept, but I refuse to give up in my efforts to help free them from the same war I once battled.

In addition to Dr. Maloney's suggestion, the push for this book came about after I was asked to speak at a meeting of parents concerned about the drug problem in their community. I found that most of them had no idea about drugs and their children. They needed information about how to keep drugs and kids apart. Using all that I had learned in this field and researching new and proven ideas, I approached Dick Lutz, my editor and publisher, about making this a reality. I am grateful that he saw the need, too.

It's my hope that after you read this book, you'll spread the word about the problems we face, young and old, if we don't stand together as a team to deal with it. Loan someone a copy of what you are about to read or direct them to where they can obtain their own. I have no doubt, that with faith and perseverance, we will be able to do our part to keep drugs and kids apart.

CONTENTS

INTRODUCTION

THE AGONY OF AN ILLNESS

Picture in your mind an illness stalking the four corners of America. An illness with the enormous power of wiping out human lives. An illness that plays no favorites to the young or the old. That makes no distinction between the rich and the poor. That sees no color. And pays no attention at all to religious or spiritual affiliation.

Visualize this disease as robbing people of their physical health. Of robbing a person of his intellect—of taking away her spiritual beliefs. A disease so subtle that it begins unnoticed and then grows to gigantic proportions in a short amount of time.

This disease has been known to take over its victims as young as nine years old. Striking one in every four humans at sometime in their life. Costing this country over 240 billion dollars a year in health care costs. Driving those under its spell to a life of self-destruction. It has caused many to commit suicide. Placing others on the road to crime. Putting others in the grip of insanity. Destroying whole families in the wink of an eye.

Imagine this illness so forceful that it corrupts the minds of all those who are stricken by it. Altering their judgment and reasoning to the point of convincing them that they are sane. A disease so cunning and powerful that it persuades those under its spell that they have no disease. That they are overcome with external conditions and not a physical, mental, and spiritual illness. An illness so cruel that it inflicts pain and suffering, not only on those that have it, but also on all those who are close to the one affected.

This disease is addiction.

THE TRUTH

Does this sound too depressing? Maybe a little over-dramatized? Scary? Hard to believe? What you have read is far from being fiction. The picture just painted is reality. All to often in this society, we see the facts about drugs and they seem to be sugar coated. Sugar coated meaning that they are looked at as "not such a big deal." Looked at as though it is a problem that may "go away" on its own.

The truth of the matter is that drugs are killing our children off at an alarming rate. The statistics have risen for years and there is no decline in sight.

Consider these facts:

- Almost 2% of sixth graders have tried marijuana.

- By the end of the 12th grade, 1/4 of students are frequent users of illegal drugs.

- Some 30% of adolescent suicides can be attributed to depression, aggravated by drug or alcohol abuse.

- The United States has the highest rate of teen-age and young adult drug abuse in the world.

Recent surveys of students have indicated that pressure to use illegal substances begins around the fourth grade.

By the age of 13, 30% of boys and 22% of girls have begun to drink alcohol.

Between the fourth and the fifth grade, the number of adolescents that experiment with alcohol, increases from 6% to 17%.

Enough said? With statistics like these, it's hard to ignore the problem. But unfortunately it often is ignored. Ignored at the point of losing more children, day after day to this terrible disease.

This disease has profound effects on not only the one affected, but the family unit and society in general.

THE FAMILY DISEASE

The use of alcohol and other drugs does not merely affect the individual under the influence, but in essence, takes others hostage as well. Family members can be pulled down by the enormous pain and suffering that chemicals inflict on their victims. Parents are often prone to blame themselves for the actions of the ones using drugs. This in itself, creates guilt and shame, leading to depression, anger, and resentments. These feelings alone, can then lead to physical problems, which in turn can then lead to a loss of faith and trust in God. This loss can be termed "Spiritual abandonment." At this end of the scale, a person's problems have only begun. And the cycle can go on and on, creating personal conflicts between each parent and other family members. It's almost as though these members of the family were, themselves, the ones to have used mood or mind altering drugs. The price that others pay for the drug induced behavior of another seems unfair and it is. But unfortunately, it still happens.

I've seen families literally torn apart by one person's drug usage. By this I mean both parents clash against one another, to the point of separation and at times, divorce. Remember, we're dealing with addiction. One of the most cunning and powerful diseases known to humankind.

Don't underestimate the force of this illness. The battle that it fights against families is wicked. The end results can leave many crippled and hurting. The confusion that is brought about can be compared to a battle. This army of destruction plays by no rules. The Geneva Convention doesn't apply. This is why it is called a "Family disease." Its effects spread to others, innocent victims. Don't misunderstand me, family members can't become chemically dependent as one would catch a cold. What **is** caught is the fallout of devastation. I liken it to being an innocent bystander when a car careens into your path, knocking you down. You then chase after this car, and in the process, fall down an open manhole. At the bottom of this manhole is a raging sewer which sweeps you off of your feet and carries you to an exit pipe that pumps you into the river. And on and on and on. Get the picture? It can be a never ending mess. And all you were was an innocent bystander.

SHAME AND GUILT

When there is any definite type of drug use or even the suspicion of drug use in the home, I can guarantee you that there will be shame and guilt. These two words are synonymous with drug abuse and addiction. They create the cycle that causes the entire family unit to plummet downhill.

Shame is the feeling of despair and disgrace. When people are ashamed, they are in a mode of feeling less than, unworthy, inadequate, and empty. The guilt can come from feeling at fault for another person's actions. *Guilt is what we feel when we think we made a mistake. Shame is what we feel when we think we are a mistake.*

Both of these feelings tend to generate a hostile barrier in dealing with the person who has the drug problem. Our society has placed such a negative stigma on chemical dependency that parents and others fear for the reputations of their families. The problem continues and shame and guilt continue to grow. It's as though one were trapped with no logical way to get out of the situation. It's this feeling of hopelessness that causes parents and others to "look the other way."

Alcohol and other drug surveys tell us that at least five other people are affected by the addiction of one person. This means not only family members, but friends and co-workers, too. The wholeness of these people is often thrown into complete chaos. Shame and guilt create a denial of the problem. And it is this denial that fuels escalation of the problem instead of searching for a solution to it. Protecting the "family name" becomes a priority.

LOOKING THE OTHER WAY

The majority of the families affected, sad to say, refrain from taking any kind of action to stop what is going on. Secrets begin to take form. Sweeping this problem under the carpet is a way to hide it from friends, co-workers, relatives, and the church. The fear is that "letting the cat out of the bag" may persuade others to look down on us. To not see the "perfect family" that so many like to portray. Shame, embarrassment, and guilt get the better of us. So much so, that rational decisions to seek help go astray. Often, family members may be in so much denial themselves, that they fail to see the root of the problem. They may think that this is a common occurrence in most other families. They have the illusion that in time this whole mess will blow over. The odds of that happening, without any outside help, is almost nil.

The feeling that one feels in a household turned upside down by chemical dependency is likened to the feeling one would get if they were forced to walk on eggshells— without breaking them. Is there a right way or a wrong way to walk on eggshells? What if they do break? How delicate should one be in doing this? The unpredictability of this situation is enormous, just as it also is in a chemically dependent household.

The situation is at most times, volatile. It's as if the entire house is resting on two tons of dynamite. The fear of being caught in a possible explosion is startling. The child with the drug problem changes, mood-wise, like a chameleon changes color. And all at the price of those so near. What a sad situation. But a preventable one, nonetheless.

GRIEF

Family members can go through grief over the sense of loss or the emotional detachment of the loved one who is using drugs. The grieving process goes through phases, such as: Denial— Anger—Bargaining—Depression, and finally—Acceptance. Acceptance being the thought that "this is just the way it is, and there is nothing I can do to change it." These steps are painful and stressful. Invisible walls are built. I like to call these walls "emotional fortresses." It's a form of mentally letting go of the problem or person, so as to not have to deal with anything even remotely painful. These fortresses are built quickly and subconsciously to protect one from the fear of "overloading," "stressing out" or "losing control". The belief that these frightening things can happen, often cause family members to question their own sanity.

I have seen countless parents who at one time or another have given up on their kids after it was discovered that they had a drug problem. The lying, stealing, cheating, negative behavior, and other drug using induced conduct was enough for these parents to feel that their kids were "out of control." Feeling that they had no recourse to get them back into control, they just disassociated themselves from them. I don't want anyone to think that this was an easy decision for any of these parents, because it wasn't. The pain, confusion, hurt, and depression that they go through first is hard to even imagine. When these same parents come to the end of the road and feel that they have no choices or alternatives, they detach and let their children go. They come to the final conclusion that their kids are going to do what they want to do. So why not let go and try to lead normal adult lives without the hassle of hassling them? I hope you noticed that I said that they felt they had no choices or alternatives. The truth of the matter is that there **are** ways and means to deal with this problem.

I often think how sad it is in this day and age, that society has so little education on the effects of drug use on children, the family system, and society. We are bombarded at times with massive information on how to deal with almost any and all problems. Except one, of course and that's chemical dependency. Parents, guardians, and all others who work with children and adolescents, and who are kept informed on this issue, will be able to recognize and take proper action to deal with it before it gets out of hand. More families could be saved and spared much pain and hurt from the grief, if only they would educate themselves to the evils of addiction. Society would be much safer and productive if it was also better informed.

This book deals with important areas that parents and others need to be knowledgeable about in order to help kids lead drug-free lives. It is intended for parents who want the best for their kids. What parent wouldn't? I'll go on to explain the 'why, when, where, and how' of drugs and kids. How to prevent them from becoming victims of drugs. How to recognize certain symptoms of drug use. The ways to get them off of drugs. And alternative ways to make them feel too worthwhile to even consider drugs. A chapter on kids and suicide is also included as this is a growing concern. I will also show you how to get involved in community action efforts to prevent drug abuse among the young.

Since drugs affect all different ages, I've made it simpler by identifying all minors as teens, kids, children, adolescents, and young people.

Gary L. Somdahl

ALCOHOL VERSUS DRUGS

Before you read any further, there is one important point to be made. This is without a doubt the most important point in this book. That is that alcohol is a drug. I'll repeat this. ALCOHOL IS A DRUG. Any substance that alters a person's mood or mind is considered a drug. And alcohol does this. The most abused drug in this country is alcohol. The fact that it is legal and so readily available makes it look acceptable and without blame. Unless you understand this and not just focus on other drugs, your labor at preventing a drug problem or dealing with a drug problem in your child is all in vain.

To make it simple and less confusing, I have used the word "drug" predominantly throughout these pages. Unless a specific type of drug is mentioned, then I am also talking about alcohol.

I

THE PARENT AS KEY PLAYER

This book isn't only about drugs and kids. It's more than that. It's about drugs and kids and how we as parents can keep them apart. It's a survival manual for us to read and study, so that we're better equipped to lead our children to drug-free lives.

One thing I've done is left out the blood and gore stories about what happens when kids and drugs mix. Most of us have already heard them. Especially if we spend any amount of time watching the evening news or reading the paper. The statistics presented throughout this book speak for themselves.

I'm often amazed at some of the parents whom I have had an opportunity to speak and listen to in the past several years. It's surprising for me to see how many of them lack the knowledge of the growing problem between kids and drugs. What's more surprising is that most have really no idea of how to educate their children so they don't ever become involved with drugs.

There is an astonishing amount of outdated information available out there. Some parents are still using it with very limited or no results. I was always taught that if nothing changes—then nothing changes. This book is about changes. It's throwing out most of what has never, or rarely, works in the field of drug prevention. There's no sense in trying the old methods if they fail to give positive results.

PAST EFFORTS

Drug prevention twenty years ago focused primarily on providing a small resource of information about the dangers of drug use. It was thought that if we gave children the knowledge of what they would be facing if they chose to get involved in drugs, this would convince them to think twice. For those whose lives were already in the belly of the beast (active drug use), maybe this would shock them back into reality and make them change their drug using behaviors. It's more than obvious that this didn't work.

Ten years ago, the strategies were assessed and changed. New and promising ideas were born. Kids were not only taught about the dangers of drugs, the fact that they could also become addicted, but they were introduced to values clarification skills. The hope was that this would turn the tide and guarantee that they would make better choices. This, too, proved to be ineffective.

The last several years has been a time for major overhauling of the entire drug prevention concept. Data was collected and reviewed and intense research was done to find out what didn't work, why it failed to work and what could be done that would be successful. One fact that stood out above all the rest was some were doing their part to try and keep drugs and kids as far apart as possible. Who were they? The schools, the police, the legal system, ministers, psychiatrists, psychologists, and others who came in contact with young people. There was one important component missing. Where were the parents?

It's fruitless to entirely depend on others to raise our children to lead drug-free lives. Sure, having support and help from anyone who's willing to give it is fine. But the bottom line is that parents are the most important people to eradicate the use of drugs by kids. It becomes obvious that you and I are the ones who have to take on the responsibility of seeing to it that our children stay away from abusing mood and mind altering chemicals. Therefore, this makes each of us key players.

KEY PLAYER DESCRIPTION

So what exactly does it mean to be a key player on your kids drug-proofing team? Let me define it for you:

Key means of importance or the person with the winning edge.

Player means the one participating or belonging with another.

Team means those associated together for the purpose of bettering their personal lives and mutual relationships.

Families are a lot like teams. They are a group of individuals related to each other with goals and common purposes for the betterment of their relationship. Each person in the family has his or her own individuality, but continues to promote and nurture each others wants and needs. At least 'healthy' families do this.

There are those family units that don't do well because they refuse to be joined together as a group. Sad to say, the children that live in these homes stand a good chance of becoming involved with drugs. Without a team spirit in the home, kids have a tendency to search other places for a feeling of belonging. All too often, they find it—in peer groups that have nothing better to do than get high.

KEY PLAYER QUALITIES

You as a parent can be the key player on your kid's drug-proofing team. The position of the key player in any sport is crucial to winning games. This player is the main and most important element because of distinctive qualities that he or she possesses. These qualities are:

One: Experience and education. The key player is well informed on certain strategies and effective plans to use to gain control of situations and turn them to advantages. The lack of control in any situation can only serve to create more dilemmas.

Sometimes situations arise out of the blue. The key player needs to be prepared to deal with any and all surprises. What may seem to be in order today, could change drastically tomorrow. The challenge of drugs is a sneaky thing. As most of us know, sometimes things don't happen the way we expect them to.

It's using our experiences from the past and changing them into viable options that will work and go a long way in preventing kids from using or abusing drugs. The more a key player knows about how to play the game and what to expect, what works and what doesn't, the more points are stacked up in his or her team's favor.

Two: The ability to play under any circumstances. Sometimes the road is hard and long ahead. It's strength and perseverance that keep a team interested in continuing to play the game, regardless of the pressures involved.

A key player keeps careful watch on the methods of the other team and does all in his or her power to stay one step ahead. The moves from the threat of drugs can be cunning and sly. They can go a long way in reversing plays, looking as though they are on the losing end, and then turning around and fighting you full force.

How often life places before us obstacles that get in the way of where we want to go. They are there to divert us from achieving what it is we hope to bring about. The stresses can be overwhelming at times. The key player continues on. Obstacles become those things that can be conquered. In fighting against them, the key player becomes only stronger and wiser and more able to overcome adverse circumstances in the future.

Three: Commitment. A winning team needs a full time player, not just a weekend warrior. The job of keeping drugs and kids apart requires a key player to be on his or her toes at all times. The possibilities of any child falling victim to drug use is too serious for a parent to ignore.

The key player has a job to do and tries different tactics if the old ones fail to work. Giving up in the face of adversity is the farthest thing from this person's mind.

All of us make committments almost everyday. Raising a drug-free child, I would hope, is a priority in any parent's life. It's hard to imagine anyone not committing to this.

Four: Unity. Teamwork is another way to describe this. Regardless of the other member's bias or attitude, on the playing field this player sees no character defects. The key player treats the rest of the team with dignity and respect and at the same time leads them to victory.

The old saying, "What we can't do alone, we can do together," goes a long way in keeping drugs and kids apart. No one has to be the 'Lone Ranger' in the battle against drug use. It's working together, side by side, that wins games.

Players who sit on the sidelines have little to contribute to their team. Sure, they may cheer their teammates along, but shouting words of encouragement doesn't get the same results as footwork does.

What would happen if Ken Griffey, Jr., told his fellow Seattle Mariners that he wished the best for them and then informed them that he would be in the clubhouse observing all nine innings? Do you really believe this would help his team? Unity involves being on the field together. It involves being a part of and not apart from.

Five: Faith and Hope. These are two words that can mean the difference between winning and losing. Without them there is no reason to put any effort whatsoever into playing the game. If we've lost faith and hope in a bright future for our children, we've lost our children. We find ourselves at the back of the line, whereas drugs stand in the front.

A key player is without a doubt that his/her team will go on to victory. It is this attitude that fills one with thoughts of winning the game before it is even played. It's a sense of visualizing the best outcome that could possibly happen before actually stepping foot on the playing field.

Miracles never happen by accident. It's believing in them first that sets them in motion. Losing sight of great possibilities is akin to giving up before the miracle happens. And it's usually just over the hill. It's faith and hope that carries the key player up this hill. It's faith in ourselves and our children and hope for their drug-free lives that carries us all beyond improbability. Faith and hope overshadow that which may seem impossible.

THE WINNER'S TEAM

Parents as key players are essential in the field of drug prevention. They hold the positive characteristics needed to make certain their children stay as far away from the menace of drugs as they can. Let's look at the difference between the characteristics of a winning team and those of a losing team:

WINNING TEAM	LOSING TEAM
Positive reinforcement	No reinforcement
Enjoys playing the game	Is easily bored
Satisfaction with teammates	Critical of teammates
High energy levels	Low energy levels
Takes control	Surrenders control
Plays to win	Plays to comply
Knows the best moves before the game	Learns the best moves after the game
Tackles all potential problems	Gives up easily

Feels close to team　　　　　　Feels far from team

In counseling young people, I can always spot which ones are from what team. **The kids on the winning team have this to say...**

"My parents care a lot about my brothers and me."

"We always do awesome things together."

"My mom admits to it when she's wrong. I see her as being human."

"Moms and Dads are supposed to love their kids, like mine love me."

"I couldn't imagine not having the support I always get from my folks."

And from those on the losing team...

"They never listen to what I have to say"

"My Father's boring. My Mom's always busy. I stay in my room most of the time."

"They're hardly ever fair. They say one thing and do another."

"I'd rather live in prison than in my own house, some times."

"Why is it they always see the mistakes I make and never the good things I do?"

It's easy to lose on the playing field. All it takes is a loss of effort on a key player's part. Nothing could be more simple. The problem is that when you lose too many games, it's hard to see anyone being interested in signing up to play when the next season rolls around. Losing innocent beautiful children to the horrors of drug use is showing a lack of initiative. You need to be on the field and put all you can into winning before you can actually hold 'the gold' in your hands.

PARENTING ISN'T FOR THE WEAK

Parents are more than simply players on the prevention field. The responsibilities that they have to take on in raising a child is often overwhelming, especially when we consider all the different roles it involves. Such as:

Educators, resources, role models, policymakers, rule setters, participants, consultants, monitors, collaborators, identifiers, confronters, interveners, managers, taxi drivers, cooks, housekeepers, reminders, alarm clocks, secretaries, janitors,

cheerleaders, referees, coaches, lenders, support-
ers, collection agencies, dispensers, nurses, friends,
heroes, security guards, nightwatch persons, de-
tectives, bankers, answering services, intermediar-
ies, locators, travel agents, employers, conductors,
delivery persons, ambassadors, repair persons,
monitors, police officers, tailors, prosecutors,
judges, and juries. You probably can think of others.

Enough said? With all the different hats that have to be
worn, is it possible to add one more—a key player? I believe it is. In fact, I believe it's absolutely essential. Especially if we have the same common goal in mind—drug-
free kids.

CATHY'S STORY

"As a single parent, it seems at times to be too much
for me to take care of my two children. I guess I never
realized how much time and effort went into raising
kids. Anyone can have a child, but it takes a special
parent to raise a child to lead a positive, happy, and
healthy life.

"The're no textbooks on the ways and means of doing this. The ways in which I was raised were the only
ways I knew in raising my children. They were all that

were known by my parents, which were learned from their parents and so on. Don't get me wrong, there were some good points in how I was raised, but there were also some things my parents neglected to teach me.

"Sure, I became involved in different drugs as I grew up. My father and mother didn't have a clue. In fact, they were very permissive in all that I did back then. Drugs became an escape for me and led me astray from the comfort of my parents. Thank God, as an adult I somehow turned it around and am very successful in what it is I do today. I lost many years growing up. Looking back, it was my involvement in drugs that contributed to throwing all that time away. Time is valuable. I can't go back and change any of it. I can change my future and make certain that my children's future doesn't turn out like my past.

"I want my kids to live a life free from drugs. I want to see them able to make decisions on their own that will keep them drug-free. It's only by breaking the pattern of past generations that I will be able to give them the right tools to do this. I often wish someone had given me the tools to drug-free living when I was a child. Now that I know what to do, there's no excuse for me to continue poor parenting practices. I will raise my kids to be the best they can be. To achieve this it takes all of us working together as a family. I believe that's what families are for."

Cathy's story illustrates the fact that we don't have to carry on the mistakes that our parents made. We need not use the same 'tools', as she called them, to raise our children to be apart from drugs. All that is needed is to change these old patterns and start anew. And when the going gets tough, hang in there, there's always a rainbow after a rain.

FIFTY WAYS TO KEEP YOUR KIDS OFF DRUGS (ACCORDING TO KIDS)

Even though this book is packed with effective and proven methods of keeping drugs and kids apart, there is one other way to learn how to be effective in keeping your kids off drugs. That's by asking the children.

In my dealing with children over the past years, I have always been curious as to what they need or want the most from their parents. After all, we have much to learn from those younger than ourselves. The best teams are those who are open-minded and willing to listen and learn. Refusing to give up until I was satisfied with what we as parents could do better, I sought these answers out wherever I went.

It's not surprising to see that those things needed the most by children are the things that can enhance their lives. All of these actions asked for, if given, have the greatest potential to build life-skills, values, morals, and positive esteem. What more could a parent hope for? Especially when a child with these traits is at the lowest risk to become involved with mood or mind altering substances.

The following fifty things that children ask for are in the exact words of each child. They are the cornerstone that a parent can and should build on.

1. Acknowledge my abilities.

2. Show unconditional love for me.

3. Show interest in my feelings.

4. Listen to me without the need to speak.

5. Spend quality time with me.

6. Show appreciation for my accomplishments.

7. Respect my opinions.

8. Allow me some quiet time.

9. Avoid giving me mixed messages.

10. Be more clear in your requests to me.

11. Participate in positive activities with me.

12. Let me express my own ideas.

13. Say that you love me, often.

14. Practice yourself what you teach to me.

15. Let me be a part of family discussions and planning.

16. Teach me how to live a healthier lifestyle.

17. Compliment me more often.

18. Reward me for good deeds.

19. Be consistent with your rules for me.

20. Treat my friends with respect.

21. Read exciting books with me.

22. Express your own feelings to me.

23. Respect my possessions and my privacy.

24. Be sensitive to my needs.

25. Show encouragement for my goals.

26. Avoid judging me.

27. Treat me fairly.

28. Be honest with me.

29. Allow me time to vent my anger.

30. Don't criticize me.

31. Help me to solve problems.

32. Show a more positive attitude towards me.

33. Laugh with me.

34. Teach me a skill that you know.

35. Be more understanding of my feelings.

36. Don't dwell on my past mistakes.

37. Teach me how to be responsible and independent.

38. Don't set unreasonable standards for me.

39. Understand that I am not perfect.

40. Recognize my talents.

41. Have faith in me.

42. Stop nagging me.

43. Don't break promises to me.

44. Be sensitive to my problems.

45. Don't ignore me.

46. Stop reminding me of what I should have done.

47. Don't tease me.

48. Have patience with me.

49. Don't compare me to others.

50. Don't insult me.

There you have it. Out of the mouths of babes. Some directions and guidelines on being the best parent you can be. And what better way to learn than from those who play on the same team as you do?

HOW TO HARM A CHILD

On the other side of the coin, there are those things that parents can do to place their child at a high risk of becoming involved with drugs. It's an almost unconscious act by some parents to actually point their kids in the wrong direction. By taking a look at what not to do, you may be better able to take a self-inventory to see that these things are not being projected from you to your son or daughter.

Don't:

Use comparison. "Why can't you be more like your cousin Zak?"

Express 'adultisms'. "When I was your age, I..." "If I were you, I would..." "Quit acting like you're a kid!"

Use putdowns. "Those earrings make you look like a whore."

Don't listen. "What was it you were saying? I wasn't listening."

Act more like a friend. "Your father really bores me. How would you deal with him if he were married to you?"

Be overly dogmatic. "Take it or leave it. That's just the way it is!" "I'm not talking about it. Discussion over!"

Be unavailable. "Sorry, honey. I'm just too busy with work to help you now. Maybe later."

Be overly protective. "Don't worry, sweetheart. I'll call your teacher in the morning and tell him why you didn't finish your assignment."

Be easy to con. "Okay, we'll agree to whatever it is you want. But just this one time."

Criticize yourself. "I'm no good as a parent. I can't do anything right."

SOME OTHER THINGS NOT TO DO

Reject your child.

Fail to accept your child.

Be cold and hard to your child.

Use coercive disciplinary methods.

Speak to your child in an abusive manner.

Be unrealistic about your child's abilities.

The use of any of these non-effective parenting skills can certainly put any child at a greater risk of being pointed in the direction of drug use. I would hope that no one uses these techniques on purpose. They are devastating to all children, whether a parent is aware they are using them or not.

THE STORY OF JAMES

He was sitting alone and huddled up to keep warm from the cold, sitting on snow-covered steps that led up to the iron grate door of a pawn shop. At fifteen years old, James lived on the streets. This was his home. The little cash he received from stealing was far too little to support his amphetamine habit.

Others may have seen him as an outcast from society, but some saw him as a victim of parents unwilling or unable to provide what parents are supposed to provide for their children.

Only thirteen, James's alcoholic father's behaviors were too much to bear. The physical and emotional abuse left scars that would take years to heal. His mother, uneducated and unmotivated, spent hours in her daily rituals of watching television, reading romance novels, and napping on the couch.

James found solace with a group of boys who had banded together as a street gang. They took him in as a member of their family. A family with their own set of rules, but nonetheless, they showed James the respect and understanding that he lacked under his own roof.

After two years of violent confrontations with warring gang members, scrapes with the law, and the rampant use of drugs, the gang split up. Most who were participants in this group had either moved away, were in jail, died, or had regained their logic and given it up. James was the lone one out.

His attempts at going back home were fruitless. His father's drinking had escalated. His mother had taken up with another man and had left. Her whereabouts were unknown.

James was assisted by a local mission in moving in with a stable family. The attention, care, and love they afforded him, led him from his life of hell to an existence of near-heaven. James' drug problem was now the only thing holding him back from a life of possibilities.

He agreed to enter a long term drug treatment center. His discharge from there after several months made a world of difference. James, by then, had learned to stand on his own two feet and make responsible decisions.

The last time I heard about James, he had enrolled in college. This now bright and articulate young man had been caught up in a war and had refused to become a casualty.

It is obvious that his original family had refused to be a team. They had chosen to seek comfort in their own selfish manner. His parents must have assumed that he was not affected by living in the mess that was his birth family. Assumptions are often wrong as were James' parents.

The family James had moved in with had made a team effort to see that he received what all children deserve— direction and support. As you can see it made a world of difference to this love-starved young man.

I hope to find James one day and see if he continued on in the positive direction in which he was moving. Will he raise his children in the competent ways that had saved his own life? I may never know the answer, but the chances are good that he carried with him what was given to him. If he does have a family today, he more than likely has brought them together as a team to win game after game on the playing field of life.

MISSION AND FULFILLMENT

There are many organizations and teams today that give structure and direction to their goals by following a mission and values statement. This is brainstormed, agreed upon, and put on paper by all members or parties involved. A mission and fulfillment statement, put together as a family priority can be both visionary and highly effective. That is, if everyone commits to follow it.

To devise a mission and fulfillment statement for your family team, sit down together to look at different goals that all of you would like to see fulfilled. Ask yourselves several questions. What is lacking in our home? What needs changing? What do we need to do to change it?

After everyone has put their two cents in and the mission and fulfillment statement is drawn up, post it in an obvious place for everyone to see. Every member of the family should review this statement as often as possible.

A mission and fulfillment statement can do wonders in bringing all members together with objectives and the means to attain them. The following is a mission and fulfillment statement to use as an example in writing your own.

MISSION AND FULFILLMENT STATEMENT

OUR MISSION

Our mission is to live together as a team with mutual respect, love, compassion, and care for each other.

WE COMMIT

We commit to support each other. Understand and accept differences. Communicate honestly. Honor each others' rights to their personal opinions. Foster attitudes that promote peace, security, and a healthy mind, body, and spirit. Be responsible for individual tasks and for assisting others when called upon. Respect for one anothers' feelings. Promote a team spirit. Listen to what others have to convey. Uphold a friendly and spirited attitude. Promote unity and closeness in our home.

WE AFFIRM

We affirm this mission and fulfillment statement as our own to fulfill a value-centered and moral family and team.

IT'S ON TO VICTORY!

BEING THE KEY PLAYER ON YOUR KID'S DRUG-PROOF-ING TEAM GIVES YOU AN ADVANTAGE OVER THE OPPOS-ING TEAM. AND THE OPPOSING TEAM THAT YOU ARE UP AGAINST IS DRUGS. REMEMBER, THIS IS A TEAM. YOUR CHILD IS PLAYING ON IT TOO. TOGETHER, WITH SUGGES-TIONS AND INFORMATION FROM THIS BOOK, YOU WILL BE MORE CAPABLE TO SUIT UP AND GO OUT ONTO THE PLAYING FIELD FOR THE WIN. YOUR OPPOSITION HAS

STRENGTH ALSO, BUT WITH CAREFUL PLANNING AND
IMPLEMENTATION OF THESE FOLLOWING FACTS, THE
POINTS WILL ALL BE IN YOUR KID'S AND YOUR FAVOR.

II

DON'T BE THE LAST TO FIND OUT

P arents always seem to be the last people on earth to discover that their kids have tried drugs or are heavily involved in them. And even then, at times, they refuse to believe this and turn a deaf ear to any information that points a finger at their children. The friends that your children hang out with are almost always sure if your kid is trying drugs or not. This is especially true if these friends are doing it along with them. Other parents find out from their own children that someone else's kids are involved in drugs. What often happens is that they keep this information from other parents for fear or guilt of breaking their own children's trust. Teachers have been known to have evidence of a child's drug use and have overlooked notifying parents, citing the rights of the student as far as anonymity and confidentiality go. And other relatives such as siblings may have knowledge and are unable to tell someone for fear of reprisals from their brother or sister or fear that their parents may not believe them in the first place.

Rumors come and rumors go and before long an entire community can have first hand knowledge that a
certain child is abusing chemicals and yet no one informs the parents. It is only when their child starts to
have academic problems, legal problems, health problems or attitude problems that they find out the worst -
that their kid is currently using some type of drug or
drugs and has been for some time. I feel sad when I see
these parents at their wits end trying to deal with a severe drug problem in their child. It would have been
much easier and saner to deal with it when it was first
recognized whether by them or someone else. The progression of this illness in young people is quick. It rarely
takes a rest or stops on its own.

LIABILITY

There is a certain liability problem for parents who
are the last to know. Their responsibility is to their children and to society in general, since these children are a
part of it also. The price that these parents pay is enormous in terms of emotional and physical health, not to
mention legal fees at times. Schools and communities
that don't tell are also liable in many ways. A child under the influence of drugs can have drastic negative effects on schools and communities. And let's not forget
the impact it has on the one using the drugs. Lives are
lost at times due to drug use. This is no insignificant

problem. Its effects can be felt by many and for a long-time down the road.

CAROL B.

Carol B., a senior student and class president, was caught at the beginning of the school year with a bottle of wine in her locker by campus security guards. Her counselor called her in and administered a drug and alcohol assessment on her. The results of this assessment showed Carol to be mildly chemically dependent and showed a recommendation of drug and alcohol treatment. A deal was struck between her and school administrators that if she discontinued her alcohol use, the matter would be dropped, she would remain class president and her parents would not be notified. Carol agreed.

Toward the end of the school year, Carol's grades and school activities had plummeted. Her parents were called in for a teacher conference and in the midst of discussion, one teacher let it be known that she had been caught with alcohol in the past and that this could be the cause of her poor academic skills. The parents were filled with rage. Not to mention the hurt and pain underneath it all. They were especially livid when told that Carol would not graduate as her credits were lacking for her to finish twelfth grade.

Three days after this conference, the principal at Carol's school received a phone call from a local attorney retained by Carol's parents. He informed the principal that unless Carol was allowed to graduate with full credits, he was prepared to file a hefty lawsuit against the school. The attorney made it clear that not only would this cost the school district thousands of dollars, but the publicity would harm it beyond repair.

When graduation time came, Carol was there in her cap and gown. She had made it out of twelfth grade . Her addiction problem by this time had progressed to a severe stage and her parents could do little to help her as she moved out of the home. Today, Carol is still using drugs. Her plans for college, a career, and a healthy happy family have fallen by the wayside. And all because someone who could have been instrumental in getting this young woman's life back on track decided to keep it a secret.

Secrets hurt people. Secrets can kill. What was this school afraid of in the first place? The loss of a student president? Looking bad? Or did they really feel that they had helped this girl by making a deal with her? There are many questions and no known answers. The fact of the matter is that Carol could have been helped in the first place by letting her parents in on what had happened when the wine was first found. The covering up or sweeping under the carpet of this one fact, resulted in the progression and further deterioration of one young life. What a shame. And to think that it could have been prevented.

I don't believe that the people involved in minimizing the problem that Carol had were consciously aware of the harm they were doing her. I do believe that they were negligent in not following through with the recommendations that the assessment showed. Also they were negligent in not letting the parents know that their daughter had been busted in school and was in need of drug and alcohol therapy. These same school officials could have also used some education themselves in chemical dependency and its effects. It's too bad that they did not know that a chemically dependent person is prone to sell his or her soul to the devil to keep their parents from finding out.

The breaking of promises and commitments is one of many signs and symptoms of dependency. Of course the people involved in the agreement with Carol that she would stop drinking, did not know that she had beat them at their own game, until it was too late. Kids with drug problems are very creative and clever in changing certain aspects of their lives so as to keep their drug use better hidden. It almost becomes a crafty game. A means of survival to better guarantee a risk free continuance of the use of drugs.

Not only schools, but law enforcement agencies can create liabilities for the community they serve by not dealing with the problem in an efficient way. This next story attests to that.

KEVIN R.

Sixteen-year-old Kevin R. was driving home from a friends house at 7:00 in the evening when blue lights started flashing behind him. After pulling to the side of the road, the police officer who had stopped him came up to his car and asked him for his license and registration. It was obvious that Kevin was under the influence of a mood and mind altering drug by the way he fumbled with the items asked for, the slurred speech, and the bloodshot eyes. The officer, noticing this and not smelling alcohol, asked Kevin if he had been smoking pot or had recently used any other type of drug. Kevin said no, and explained to the officer that he had been speeding because he was slightly late in getting home. He went on to explain that his parents were strict and that he feared being grounded for a long stretch of time.

The officer felt sympathy for him but warned Kevin that if he ever caught him again speeding or being in the condition he was in, he would arrest him. The officer returned to his car and Kevin drove off. Two miles down the road, Kevin's car went over the center line and collided with a car traveling in the opposite direction. The accident was fatal to the other driver, a 56 year old businessman with a wife and three children. Kevin was slightly injured and after spending one week in a hospital, he was charged with vehicular homicide and convicted.

Had the police officer who stopped this young man realized that anyone under the influence of a drug is a liability to themselves and others, this tragedy could have been averted. If Kevin had been arrested at the traffic stop he may have been required by the court system to complete a drug and alcohol assessment and to follow any recommendations for help. True, Kevin could have been persuaded by the legal system to seek help and still been involved in a drug related accident in a week or a month later. Recognizing a drug problem and making sure that this person goes through the system to remedy it, is no guarantee that all will be well. But ignoring it in the first place is irresponsible and places an innocent public at risk.

In no way am I placing the blame on the police or the schools for a person's actions under the influence of drugs.

Anyone who places themselves in these positions is totally responsible and should suffer any family or legal consequences. If those who had firsthand knowledge of these young people abusing any type of chemical had intervened in the beginning, any trouble later on may have been prevented.

DWAYNE T.

Fifth grader Dwayne T. enjoyed the social activities that his parents were involved in. Every Saturday evening they would invite several of their friends over to their home for cards, conversation, and drinks. This year they had come to a mutual agreement to allow Dwayne one mixed drink during this weekly event. They made it plain to him that it would be one drink and no more.

One Friday night, Dwayne came in late from a school basketball game and reeked of alcohol. His parents, upset, sat down with him and explained why they were concerned. They let him know that the permission given him to drink one drink per week at home was so he would not have to drink elsewhere. They honestly felt that this would satisfy his curiosity for alcohol and as he was in the home, he was safe from developing an alcohol problem.

Dwayne continued to drink his one token drink each Saturday night but kept secret his thirst and consumption of alcohol outside of the home too. His parents were proud of the fact that they had made a responsible decision. They had no idea that this decision would backfire later.

It was in the middle of January that Dwayne returned home from a party with his friends, where he had consumed a large quantity of beer and hard liquor. In fact he was so intoxicated that two of his older pals carried him to his front porch. Fearing that Dwayne's parents would also find them inebriated, they rang the doorbell and swiftly drove off. What they did not realize was that Dwayne's mother and father were out shopping. When they returned home two hours after their son had been delivered to their front door, they found their son lying on the front porch dead from exposure to the bitter cold.

Parents who have the illusion that they are doing their kids a service by supplying alcohol or other drugs to them in a safe environment are not in touch with reality. Show me a kid that is allowed freedom to drink at home and I will almost always be able to show you the same kid doing the same thing, outside the home. Allowing kids to use any type of mood or mind altering chemicals is to set them up for major problems in the future.

THE BIG BANG

Anyone that is under the effects of any kind of drug is a liability. And it is the responsibility of all parties to not be a part of this liability, but to try and prevent it. Providing drugs, choosing not to look, or sweeping it under the carpet is to do more harm than good. It is like finding a ticking time bomb and placing it on your bedside table so you will remember to call the bomb squad when you wake up in the morning. The only problem being that if this bomb detonates in the middle of the night, you may not wake up. This may sound a little farfetched, but the hard, cold fact is that when nothing is done for kids using drugs, it is only a matter of time until the explosion occurs. And the fallout can be detrimental for others as well.

It's easy now to see how keeping secrets can bring about destruction to human lives. And it's all brought about in order to protect the person using drugs. How many people would actually protect a person responsible for hurting countless others and is unpredictable in what his or her actions may be next? Who in their right mind would keep secret and fail to help a friend with a life-threatening illness? Most people would jump at the first opportunity to help and to assist. Why does it seem so hard when it involves a person in bondage from drugs? The answer is simple. Today, many people still view someone abusing or addicted to chemicals as weak. They feel the need to protect this person at any cost to save them the humiliation, shame, and embarrassment of others finding out. There is a sincere need to save this person's reputation, whatever it may take. And let's not forget the fact that the one playing Superman has very little idea how dangerous and addictive drugs are. He or she fails to understand the power that chemicals can have. Nor do they see that ignoring drug use is totally ineffective.

KATIE B.

Her father thought little about the fact that he had caught her in the garage with a gasoline soaked towel held up to her face. He joked about it and even told some stories of how he had done almost the exact same thing when he was her age.

When Katie's mother found out later that evening what Katie had been doing, she was concerned. After confronting her husband, she suggested that they make an appointment for Katie to see a psychologist, as she viewed this as abnormal behavior. The husband finally convinced her that this was just a passing fad that their daughter was going through. He also expressed that the family's good standing in the community could be hurt if others found out that their daughter was seeing a mental health professional. The mother relented reluctantly.

Two months after this conversation, Katie went into a seizure and was transported by ambulance to the hospital. The strong odor of gasoline from her skin hung in the air of the emergency room. The doctor in charge, explained to Katie's parents that the inhaled gas fumes had created extensive damage to their daughter's brain. Irreversible damage.

There are a lot of "could-a, should-a, and would-a's" in this story. Had this young girl's parents been better informed and more willing to help, this more than likely would not have turned out the way it did. The liability factor would have been eliminated or lessened.

Being a key player on your kid's drug-proofing team reduces the risk of liability. It takes the big bang out of your life and his/hers. It places you strategically in position to play the game with an effective plan, and not alone. Remember that your child also plays on your team, and together with strong teamwork, the chances of winning are heightened. No more secrets. No more having to turn a deaf ear. No more worrying over whether your child knows about the dangers of drugs or not. The queasy feeling of beinq uncomfortable talking about this subject does not have to be there. A team plays by the rules and knows the correct moves to make.

PAYING CLOSE ATTENTION

Educating yourself about what to look for, in order to make a determination as to if your child is using drugs is paramount to prevention. It doesn't take a skilled scientist to find this out. In fact it's relatively simple. But it often involves paying close attention. Some kids who use drugs are blatant about it. Their actions and behaviors speak out loud—"I am on drugs!" They can be spotted in a crowd. Others are more conscious of their behaviors. They usually take great pains to attempt to appear normal or sober. And especially around their parents or anyone in authority. These are the ones that require close observation. Those who abuse or are addicted to drugs can hide the effects only to a certain extent. They are much like counterfeit money. From a distance it looks like legal tender. But a close-up look reveals flaws that tip you off that it's bogus.

If you spot any of the following signs and symptoms in your kid, don't panic and begin to yell "Fire!" Keep in mind that some of these behaviors, at certain times, are normal in the child and adolescent years. This includes conduct such as: A lack of motivation, anger, mood swings, etc. A reoccurrence of any of these may indicate a possible abuse or addiction problem. The majority of drug-related behaviors are not normal. These include: Dilated pupils, drug graffiti, the discovery of drugs and paraphernalia, etc. These are almost definite signs of a problem.

PHYSICAL SYMPTOMS

ANY UNUSUAL GAIN OR LOSS IN WEIGHT.
Especially if it is rapid.

UNEXPLAINED CUTS OR BRUISES
Including any reoccurring injuries.

POOR CONCENTRATION AND ATTENTION
SPAN

THE EXCESSIVE USE OF EYE DROPS, DECONGES
TANTS, BREATH MINTS, GUM , AND CO-
LOGNE

MEMORY LAPSES
Short term or long term memory.

INDIFFERENCE TO HYGIENE AND GROOMING
Especially if it is a drastic change.

SLURRED OR INCOHERENT SPEECH

EXTREME SILENCE OR STARING OFF INTO
SPACE

BLOODSHOT EYES OR DILATED PUPILS
Includes glazed eyes and droopy eyelids.

THE NEGLECT OF APPEARANCE
Especially a sudden change. Includes hair,
make-up, jewelry, and clothing.

TATTOOS OF ANY KIND
Definitely if of marijuana leaf, drug slang, etc.

CARVING OF INITIALS, WORDS, OR ART INTO
ANY PART OF THE BODY

POOR CONCENTRATION AND ATTENTION SPAN

INFLAMMATION OF THE NOSE AND EYELIDS

EXTREMES IN ENERGY
Either jumpy, hyper, nervous or sluggish,
slow, dull.

SICKNESS
Vomiting, diarrhea, headaches, upset stomach,
double or blurred vision, cough.

DRASTIC APPETITE CHANGE
Reduction or increase in food intake.

EMOTIONAL SYMPTOMS

DEPRESSION
Includes threats of or attempts at suicide.

CONFUSION

EXTREME MOOD SWINGS

ANGER, HOSTILITY, OR IRRITABILITY

LACK OF MOTIVATION
Laziness or low self-esteem.

SELF-PITY

SADNESS
Includes verbal statements of hopelessness.

BEHAVIORAL SYMPTOMS

DISHONESTY

LACK OF INTEREST IN ACTIVITIES AND HOBBIES

SECRETIVENESS

KNOWLEDGEABLE ABOUT THE LOCATION
SITES OF LOCAL PARTIES

UNACCOUNTABLE SPENDING OF MONEY
Includes withdrawals from bank account.

UNACCOUNTABLE POSSESSION OF SUMS OF
MONEY

FAVORABLE ATTITUDE TOWARD DRUGS
Pro-legalization views and defending drug use.

ABUSIVENESS
Any violence or abuse against people, animals
or property. This includes emotional, verbal, and
physical abuse.

EXTREME CHANGE IN SLEEP HABITS
Lack of sleep or oversleeping.

USE OF CANDLES, INCENSE, OR ROOM
DEODORIZERS TO HIDE ODORS
Also, any odors not familiar.

ANY DRUG GRAFFITI ON NOTEBOOKS, PAPER,
WALLS, OR CLOTHES

WRITTEN DRUG SLOGANS, POEMS, OR PHRASES

DRUG RELATED MAGAZINES, POSTERS, CURIOS,
VIDEOS, OR MUSIC

VERBAL RECITATION OF DRUG RELATED SONGS
OR POEMS

SPIRITUAL SYMPTOMS

REDUCTION IN CHURCH OR YOUTH GROUP
ACTIVITIES

DRASTIC CHANGE IN MORALS AND VALUES

A CHANGE FROM BELIEF TO NON-BELIEF IN
GOD

PROFANITY

INVOLVEMENT IN SATANISM, WITCHCRAFT, AND SORCERY

Different drugs can cause different effects in kids. Also, the amount used and frequency of use can bring on different signs and symptoms. This list will serve as a guide in identifying a possible drug use problem in your child. This is only intended to confirm any suspicions you may have. As a key player, you will need to follow through with a drug and alcohol assessment by a trained professional to receive a definite diagnosis. I'll talk about this later in this book.

Signs and symptoms can also be broken down into certain other areas of a young person's life. Some of these areas involve other people who may notice a problem with your child before you do. It is my hope that if they do, they will let you in on what they see.

FAMILY SYSTEM

DEFIANCE OF HOUSE RULES AND AGREEMENTS
Includes chores and commitments.

THE REJECTION OR QUESTIONING OF FAMILY VALUES

SECRECY OF WHEREABOUTS, ACTIONS,
POSSESSIONS, AND ACTIVITIES

ANY AVOIDANCE OR BEING UNCOMFORTABLE
ABOUT DISCUSSIONS OF DRUGS

EXCESSIVE TIME SPENT IN BEDROOM, BATH-
ROOM, OR GARAGE

GENETIC PREDISPOSITION
Any family history of chemical dependency
places a child at risk.

SCHOOL SYSTEM

HOMEWORK AND OTHER ASSIGNMENTS NOT
COMPLETED

A NEGATIVE ATTITUDE ABOUT SCHOOL

LOSS OF INTEREST IN SPORTS OR CLUB
MEMBERSHIP

UNEXCUSED TARDINESS OR ABSENTEEISM

A MARKED DROP IN GRADES

DISCIPLINARY PROBLEMS WITH TEACHERS OR STAFF

FALLING ASLEEP IN CLASS

ASSOCIATION WITH KNOWN DRUG-USING STUDENTS

LEGAL SYSTEM

ANY ARRESTS FOR BEING UNDER THE INFLUENCE OR POSSESSION OF ANY TYPE OF DRUG OR DRUG PARAPHERNALIA

AUTO ACCIDENTS

THEFT OF FAMILY POSSESSIONS OR MONEY

LOITERING WITH KNOWN DRUG USERS

SOCIAL SYSTEM

A CHANGE IN FRIENDS

SECRECY ABOUT CERTAIN FRIENDS

NOT INVITING CERTAIN FRIENDS TO HOUSE

LATE NIGHT ACTIVITIES WITHOUT
    ACCOUNTABILITY

SECRETIVE PHONE CALLS

PROMISCUITY

ANY ASSOCIATION WITH DRUG-USING PEERS

If your child shows any of these signs and symptoms
to any degree, it is safe to presume that they are involved
with some type of drug. It is possible that your suspicions will be wrong. But it is always safer to react to
your suspicions than to ignore them. An ounce of prevention could save a life.

CROSSING THE STREET

Do you remember what your parents taught you
about crossing the street in your childhood years? How
they pointed out that the vehicles driving back and forth
may not see you and not be able to stop on time? That a
bad accident could be avoided if you followed three
simple rules? Do you remember what those three rules
that could spare your life were?

STOP!

Find the crosswalk before crossing any street. Don't jaywalk or cross between parked cars. Stand on the sidewalk and not the street portion.

LOOK!

Before stepping off of the sidewalk, look first to your left and then to your right. Be very observant.

LISTEN!

Keep your ears in tune for any sounds that would indicate that a vehicle was coming. Then proceed across the street.

These are the basic rules of how to save your life in doing something as simple as walking from one side of the street to the other. They're as elementary as ABC. Using these same rules can also work in spotting drug use.

STOP!

Take time out from your daily activities. Don't become so caught up in what you're doing that you avoid being mindful of what others are doing.

LOOK!

Be observant. Watch for attitudes and actions. Take notice of any extreme changes. Sometimes the obvious is right in front of your face.

LISTEN!

Keep your ears peeled to the mode of speech. Listen closely to what is being said. What your kid's friends have to say can be filled with important clues.

Stop, look, and listen. Who would have ever thought that this old lifesaver could pave the way for a drug-free life? It's plain rules like this that can give a key player the right method needed to win the game. And it's so uncomplicated.

BAD NEWS

Still comfortable with the thought that there is no way your kid or others could hide the abuse or addiction of drugs from you? Consider the following bad news.

There are approximately 4 million adolescents currently chemically dependent.

Studies show that 1 in 4 adolescents who experiment with any type of drug today may become chemically dependent at some time in the future.

It often takes only 6 to 18 months of heavy drug use for an adolescent to become chemically dependent.

Drug impaired driving is the leading cause of death for young people between the ages of 15 and 24.

I have never met a parent who has told me that they are relieved their child is an addict. That they have always had a goal in life to make sure that they were always provided with the best drugs there are. Absurd? Yes! No one wants a child of theirs to experiment, abuse, or become dependent on any chemical. But yet some young person somewhere out there is becoming involved in some type of drug as you read this. Who knows who it is or who it will be in the next minute?

DIFFERENT DRUG—SAME RESULT

I stated earlier that alcohol is a drug. It has the same potential outcome as any other type of mind or mood altering drug—addiction. Prescription medications have the same potential outcome if used beyond the recommended dosage—addiction. Plants, such as poppies, that grow in your backyard or in the window sill of a living room may also have the same potential outcome —addiction. The clearest way that I can say this is that "a drug is a drug is a drug is a drug." It may have a different name but it still has the potential for turning one's life upside down.

To further your training in being the best key player around, I have listed below some of the most commonly abused drugs by young people. The more education that you as a parent have on all aspects of signs, symptoms, and different drugs, the better equipped you will be to head off a disaster.

One other reason that I have decided to include a description of different drugs is because parents need to know what they look like. I receive calls every week from parents who find pills, leafs, powders, and other foreign substances in their kid's bedrooms. They have no idea whether these substances are dangerous or not. Becoming knowledgeable on the wide array of chemicals that are available today to young people gives your team the winning margin.

STIMULANTS

NICOTINE

Methods of use: Oral, smoked.
Watch for: Cigarettes, cigars, chewing tobacco, snuff, pipes.
Causes: Increased heart rate, rise in blood pressure.
Names: Smokes, snuff, chew.

COCAINE

Methods of use: Injected, inhaled.
Watch for: White or yellow powder.
Causes: Increased breathing, heart rate and
temperature, insomnia, loss of appetite,
paranoia, seizures. Can cause death by
cardiac arrest or respiratory failure.
Names: Coke, snow, blow.

CRACK COCAINE

Methods of use: Smoked.
Watch for: White or tan pellets or small rocks that
look like soap.
Causes: Increased breathing, heart rate and
temperature, insomnia, loss of appetite,
paranoia, seizures. Can cause death by
cardiac arrest or respiratory failure.
Names: Crack, rock, freebase.

AMPHETAMINES

Methods of use: Oral, injected, inhaled.
Watch for: Tablets, pills, capsules.
Causes: Increased heart rate, breathing, and body
temperature.
Names: Speed, uppers, Benzedrine, Dexedrine,
Biphetamine.

METHAMPHETAMINES

Methods of use: Oral, injected, inhaled.
Watch for: White or yellow powder, pills, rocks that
        resemble a block of paraffin.
Causes: Increased heart rate, breathing, and body
        temperature.
Names: Crank, crystal meth, speed, ice.

Additional information

Stimulants can also cause headaches, sweating, diz-
ziness, blurred vision, and anxiety. Extreme doses can
cause an irregular heartbeat, lack of coordination, agi-
tation, and hallucinations. Some of these reactions can
lead to strokes and possible death.

DEPRESSANTS

ALCOHOL

Methods of use: Oral.
Watch for: Beer, wine, wine coolers, distilled spirits.
Causes: Intoxication, disoriented behavior, memory
        loss. High doses can cause respiratory
        failure and possible death.
Names: Booze, cold one.

BARBITURATES

Methods of use: Oral, injected.
Watch for: Yellow, red, blue, or red and blue capsules, liquid, soluble powder.
Causes: Slurred speech, altered perceptions. High doses can cause respiratory failure, coma, and possible death.
Names: Downers, barbs, Seconal, Nembutal, Amytal, Tuinal.

BENZODIAZEPINES

Methods of use: Oral, injected.
Watch for: Tablets, capsules.
Causes: Slurred speech, altered perceptions. High doses can cause respiratory failure, coma, and possible death.
Names: Librium, Valium, Equanil, Miltown, Serex, Tranxene.

Additional information

Depressants slow down functions of the body. They impair judgment and create the loss of inhibitions. Combining alcohol with the use of depressants is extremely dangerous and can cause death.

HALLUCINOGENS

LSD

Methods of use: Oral.
Watch for: Tablets, powder, liquid, blotter paper.
Causes: Hallucinations, distorted perceptions.
Names: Acid, microdot, blotter acid.

MESCALINE/PEYOTE

Methods of use: Oral, injected.
Watch for: Tablets, capsules, brown discs, mush
        rooms.
Causes: Hallucinations, distorted perceptions.
Names: Mesc, buttons, shrooms.

PCP

Methods of use: oral, injected, inhaled, smoked
        (sprinkled on marijuana).
Watch for: Tablets, liquid, rock crystal.
Causes: Hallucinations, distorted perception,
        agitation.
Names: Angel dust, hog.

CANNABIS

MARIJUANA

Methods of use: Oral, smoked.
Watch for: Dried parsley looking, leafs, stems, seeds.
Causes: Difficulty in concentration, impaired
      perceptions, increased appetite, lack of
      motivation.
Names: Pot, reefer, grass, weed, dope.

HASH

Methods of use: Oral, smoked.
Watch for: Black or brown dried chunks, thick liquid.
Causes: Difficulty in concentration, impaired
      perceptions, increased appetite, lack of
      motivation.
Names: Hash, hash oil.

Additional information

Cannabis can impair short term memory and the ability to comprehend. It alters the sense of time and distance and reduces the ability to concentrate.

NARCOTICS

MORPHINE

Methods of use: Oral, injected, smoked.
Watch for: White crystals, tablets, liquid.
Causes: Anxiety, nausea, drowsiness.
Names: M, dope, Pectoral syrup.

OPIUM

Methods of use: Oral, smoked, injected.
Watch for: Powder, brown chunks.
Causes: Anxiety, nausea, drowsiness.
Names: Dover's powder, Paregoric, Parepectolin.

CODEINE

Methods of use: Oral, injected.
Watch for: Capsules, tablets, liquid.
Causes: Anxiety, nausea, drowsiness.
Names: Empirin compound with codeine, Tylenol
        with codeine, cough medicine with codeine.

MEPERIDINE

Methods of use: Oral, injected.
Watch for: Tablets, powder, liquid.

Causes: Anxiety, nausea, drowsiness.
Names: Pethidine, Demerol, Mepergan.

HEROIN

Methods of use: Injected, smoked, inhaled, oral.
Watch for: White or brown powder, tarlike substance.
Causes: Anxiety, nausea, drowsiness.
Names: Smack, junk, black tar, dope, stuff, H.

METHADONE

Methods of use: Oral, injected.
Watch for: Liquid.
Causes: Anxiety, nausea, drowsiness.
Names: Medicine, methadone, Dolophine, Amidone.

PERCOCET   FENTANYL
DARVON   PERCODAN
TUSSIONEX   LOMOTIL
TALWIN

Methods of use: Oral, injected.
Watch for: Tablets, capsules, liquid.
Causes: Anxiety, nausea, drowsiness.
Names: As listed above.

Additional information

Narcotics also produce restlessness and a going in and out of consciousness. High doses can cause respiratory failure, coma, and possible death.

ANABOLIC STEROIDS

Methods of use: Oral, injected.
Watch for: Tablets, capsules, liquid.
Causes: Increased body weight, and strength, acne,
        aggressive behavior.
Names: Steroids, roids.

Additional information

Anabolic steroids are often used by athletes and body-builders. These drugs can have over 70 different side effects for the user, including sterility and impotence. Some side effects show up years later, such as heart failure and strokes.

INHALANTS

Methods of use: Inhaled.
Watch for: Aerosols, paints, cleaning solvents,
            Whiteout, glue, gasoline, propellants.

Causes: Nausea, sneezing, coughing, nosebleeds,
    fatigue, loss of coordination, headaches.
Names: Different name brands associated with above
    "watch for" list.

Additional information

The inhalation of various vapors can also cause extreme violent behavior, seizures, brain damage, and possible death.

DESIGNER DRUGS

ANALOGS OF MEPERIDINE

Methods of use: Inhaled, injected.
Watch for: White powder.
Causes: Anxiety, nausea, drowsiness.
Names: Synthetic heroin, MPTP, MPPP, PEPAP.

ANALOGS OF FENTANYL

Methods of use: Inhaled, injected.
Watch for: White powder.
Causes: Anxiety, nausea, drowsiness.
Names: Synthetic heroin, china white.

ANALOGS OF AMPHETAMINES/METHAMPHET-
    AMINES

Methods of use: Oral, injected, inhaled.
Watch for: Tablets, capsules, white powder.
Causes: Increased heart rate, breathing, and body
        temperature.
Names: MDMA (Essence, Adam, XTC, Ecstasy),
        MDM, STP, EVE, DOB, DOM, TMA, 2 & 5-DMA,
        PMA.

ANALOGS OF PHENCYCLIDINE

Methods of use: Oral, injected, smoked.
Watch for: Tablets, capsules, liquid.
Causes: Increased body weight, and strength, acne,
        aggressive behavior.
Names: Steroids, roids.

Additional information

Designer drugs are drugs made underground, often
in home based labs. The chemists making these drugs
modify the molecular structure of certain types of illegal drugs to produce analogs. These analogs are what
are termed 'designer drugs.'

Most of these analogs are several times more powerful than the actual drugs and can cause severe brain
damage and possible death.

LEGAL VS. ILLEGAL DRUGS

As you have probably noticed not all of the above named drugs are illegal. There are many types of drugs that affect the body, mind, or behavior that are legal. Prescription drugs are considered legal and safe only when used under the direction of a physician for the person they are intended for. And only if used according to the directions that go along with them.

As a key player on your kid's drug-proofing team, I hope this list will give you insight into certain behaviors that your child may exhibit. It will also help you in determining what drug your child may be using. But remember, a drug is a drug is a drug. Any drug is potentially harmful to a young person, whether it is a street drug, alcohol, prescription drug, or even an aerosol product found under the kitchen sink.

ONCE UPON A TIME ...

We all love fairy tales. These stories of fiction play an important role in each of our lives as well as our children. They teach us valuable morals and values and show the difference between right and wrong. Fairy tales are both entertaining and educational.

But some tall tales lead us down dark roads. They illustrate wrong messages that can and often are construed as reality, or the truth. Many fairy tales are circulating among all of us that are concerned about the impact of drugs on young lives. The bad thing is that they are often erroneous and give false messages about the effects and dangers of using chemicals and getting high. It is here that I want to dispel these inaccurate tales and turn them into the truth.

OLD TALES AND MODERN REALITY

Fairy tale: **"It's only beer."**

Reality: Alcohol is the common ingredient in all alcoholic beverages. Beer can cause intoxication, lead to abuse, addiction, and is also often fatal.

Fairy tale: **"I'm relieved it's only alcohol and not drugs."**

Reality: Alcohol is a mind and mood altering drug. It depresses the central nervous system, slowing down bodily functions such as heart rate, pulse, and respiration.

Fairy tale: **"People are friendlier when they drink."**

Reality: People are also more hostile, more dangerous, more criminal, more homicidal, and more suicidal.

A significant percentage of all murders and suicides are alcohol related.

Fairy tale: **"One or two drinks never hurt any one."**

Reality: Drinking and driving is a serious problem with teens. Even in small amounts, alcohol slows reaction time, reduces coordination, and impairs eyesight. One or two drinks may be enough to cause a fatal accident.

Fairy tale: **"Kids can't become addicted at that young of an age."**

Reality: Addiction or chemical dependency can affect anyone, regardless of age, sex, race, social or economic status. Because of the lack of emotional and physical maturity, addiction can develop rapidly in young people sometimes within six months after the initial use of a drug.

Fairy tale: **"Getting high is funny."**

Reality: Maybe in old Charlie Chaplin and W.C. Fields movies, but hardly in real life. Being high is no funnier than any other illness, handicap, or incapacity.

Fairy tale: **"Controlling the use of drugs is safe."**

Reality: The control of any drug only lasts so long. It is only a matter of time before the drug controls the one taking it.

Fairy tale: **"I've seen people quit anytime they want to."**

Reality: The fact that someone quits and goes back to using again, shows how powerful addiction can be. It has the capability of convincing the addict that they don't have a problem.

Fairy tale: **"Honest, dedicated hard working people seem to be able to use drugs with no problems."**

Reality: They have had no problems, yet! We all
   have yets in our lives. If it has not
   happened—it has not happened yet.

Fairy tale: **"Children in time, all grow out of their
problems."**

Reality: It is not possible to grow out of having
   a disease. The use of drugs compounds problems and tends to create
   more havoc later in life.

So, there you have it. Fairy tales turned into reality. I
am always astounded at the misinformation that is presented and believed today by parents. It is no fault of
any one person. The tall tales concerning kids and drugs
have been handed down for generations and generations. That cycle can now be broken. The parent who is
a key player on their kid's drug-proofing team has a
responsibility to learn the truth and use it in winning
on the field.

IF DRUGS ARE SO BAD...WHY DO KIDS
USE THEM?

As I promised earlier in this book, I will try and explain the 'why' of kids using drugs. Knowing that literally all types of drugs can harm and erode their physical, mental, and spiritual well-being, what would cause them to experiment or abuse chemicals? There is no easy answer. After years of talking to and asking drug-using kids 'why?'—these are the most frequent answers that I get:

FOR	DUE TO	TO BE
Excitement	Low esteem	Sociable
Fun	Loneliness	Popular
Relaxation	Depression	Rebellious
Curiosity	Peer pressure	Cool

Has the psychological make-up of today's youth changed in such a drastic genetic way from past years? Were those born in the past era more intelligent? More moral? Did they have some mental power that is lacking in young people, today? The answer is emphatically 'no'.

SOCIAL PRESSURES

The stage for drug use is set by influence. Influence is the power to directly or indirectly sway, affect, or impact an individual. This can be in a positive and stimulating way or in a negative and dangerous way.

So, what are these factors or influences that are leading the youth of today to make such poor choices in their lives? Let's take a look at them.

THE REMOTE CONTROL SOCIETY

Today we live in an instant gratification society. Just about all that we need or want is literally at our fingertips. Patience has become a virtue of the past. We can pick up the phone and have what it is we may desire delivered to our front doorstep within the hour. This is what I like to call the "I want it—and I want it now" generation. Instead of stopping to smell the flowers, we tend to trample them as we run to get to where it is we want to go. And when we get there, it often isn't where we want to be. So we try again. And again. And again.

Just as we learn that a simple aspirin will relieve a simple headache, we learn also, that a simple cocktail or shot of bourbon can relieve stress. Different colors and sizes of pills for different maladies can take away in an instant—whatever it is that ails us. It's that easy. Even Little Alice in Wonderland can attest to this. She knew enough to know that one drink could make her smaller and another could make her taller.

Kids know, as little Alice did, that certain chemicals can change the way they feel. And in an instant. There's no waiting in line, no waiting for the mail, no watching the clock. Drugs are fast acting. Once ingested in the system, they almost immediately change the way one feels.

THE SOLUTION TO LIFE'S PROBLEMS — ADVERTISEMENTS

Ads are geared to let us know that we can look better, feel better, do better, and be better—but only if we buy their product. They tend to place guilt on the fact that some of us lead mediocre lives. That we need more gusto or better clothes or a better hairdo in order to survive as humans. The ads constantly cry out, "Buy this and be better than anyone else!" But, do we really need to be better? What's the matter with 'just' the way we are?

Television, radio, and printed ads are mostly directed to a younger audience. And this means ads that push cigarettes and alcohol. Their sexy contents powerfully push the message home—"Be who you always wished you could be." The alcohol and tobacco industry spend billions of dollars a year on these messages. Open any magazine, turn the TV channel to a sporting event, read the sides of city buses, check out the billboards, and look at the massive and impressive store displays.

Kids are inspired by these smooth and grand messages. They seem to quietly whisper to the youngster whose attention is drawn to them—"Follow me."

Over the counter medications are also a big sell. Products are peddled to take away the pain, lose weight, sleep better, have more energy, and cure thousands of other ailments. It's all meant to let each of us know that the change we all demand (according to advertisers) can come in a nicely wrapped bottle, box, or package.

MUSIC, MOVIES, AND MADNESS

The messages may seem subtle, but to young minds they have powerful effects. Kids use music as an escape from stress, anger, and boredom. This can be a relaxing way to escape from the harsh realities of the real world, but it can also lead them into harsher and more damaging realities. There are some great songs out there that have beautiful melodies and lyrics. And there are songs that glorify and esteem negative lifestyles. In fact it has come to where some recording companies put ratings on their compact discs and tapes. But if parents aren't aware of what their kids are listening to and fail to read the lyrics or listen themselves, then what's the point?

Kids have bundles of disposable money that goes to the purchase of music. Record stores make a killing off of them. Don't get me wrong, some artists put out songs with redeeming qualities that can actually help build a young person's life. But the dark side of music still grabs the attention of many. Especially the attention of someone who has low self-worth and feels more comfortable feeding into lyrical messages that affirm feelings of gloom and desolation.

Movies can have the same effects as music. They often have been known to glamorize sex, drug use, violence, and hatred. The lack of values and morals on the screen tend to show kids that it's not such a big deal to go off the path of virtue and to take dangerous chances with life. Kids identify well with actors and actresses and want to play the part themselves no matter what it takes. I'd be willing to bet that the majority of kids could name off ten well known movie stars more accurately than they could name ten past presidents.

THE ROLE OF BAD ROLE MODELS

Role models and heroes have always had a gigantic influence on the younger generation. This is good. We all need someone to reflect on, to show us that the impossible is not really impossible. There are many great heroes out there, including fantasy mentors, cartoon characters, biblical notables, school teachers, etc. The list is endless. We get so immersed in their lives that we follow in their footsteps. And this is wonderful,

unless, of course, these footsteps lead from initially over-
coming the improbable to giving up and calling it quits.

Some heroes make mistakes. We all do, and I won't
dispute that. But when a hero, such as a sports legend,
admits to drug use and down-plays the seriousness of
it, the message our kids hear, is that drug use is no big
concern. They see countless people that are put up on a
pedestal, and then fall, as a result of drug abuse and
sometimes addiction. Then they often see the same hero
rise up out of the ashes to become more successful and
more popular than they were before. The message
communicated to young people is that even if one were
to do drugs, they can always opt to change their lives
later and go on. This message may not sound all that
bad for someone caught in the clutches of addiction,
but it conveys the notion that drug use, now, is not a
big deal. It says "Use now—become more successful
later."

TELEVISION—THE GREAT AMERICAN GHOST

Much has been said from other experts about excessive exposure to television by kids. The boob tube has
little social redeeming value in it. Like movies, television has a dramatic influence on young lives. Even more
so than films. It's more accessible and cheaper. That

harmless looking screen that sits in the living room of virtually every American home contains all of the above influences that I have just described: Advertisements for instant relief from this life, horrible heroes, music that leaves out morals and values, movies that attempt to prove that wrong is right, and a long list of shows that try to prove that 'sex' is what living is all about.

Television can also be described as "The great American baby-sitter." A large share of parents use it to pacify the boredom instilled in some kids. Little do they know that it is doing more harm and creating more boredom for them than they realize. There are some shows that are educational and highly enlightening for young minds. Unfortunately they seem to be in the minority. By the time a person becomes an adult, they have witnessed thousands of violent acts, and other negative scenes that inevitably leave some impression on the mind. Sitting for hours in front of the screen has a tendency to unmotivate the young. It's used all too often as an escape from responsibility.

THE DISPOSABLE FAMILY... (OR THE FARMING OUT OF OUR KIDS)

Dysfunction in the home, parental drug abuse, inconsistent discipline, violence, the lack of structure, and a loss of values and morals, places children out of control. It puts them in position to turn to chemicals to ease the pain, hurt, and loneliness of not feeling good enough. Some parents have given up hope of ever seeing their kid's self-esteem make a comeback. Instead of becoming part of the solution, they are moving their children out of the immediate home and into the homes of others—with the belief that things will get better.

I am saddened when I see a beautiful young face in my office that lists the moves to different homes that they have had to endure. One child described his move to his father's house (the parents were divorced) in another state. After two months, he was sent to his uncle's house in yet another state. Three months later, he was returned to his mother's home, only to be sent back to his father's home, three weeks later. This game of childhood yo-yo is devastating, demeaning, and cruel to kids. It also puts them at a high risk of ingesting drugs to deal with the confusion and turmoil.

GOING AGAINST THE GRAIN—PEER PRESSURE

There are a lot of misconceptions about peer pressure today. So many of us tend to believe it is when one kid or a group of kids threaten, coerce, or pull another kid into doing what he or she does not want to do. This does happen at times, but not as often as many may believe. Peer pressure can be silent. It can be an emotional force that tempts a person to go along with the rest, or feel like the odd man out.

Kids love to belong. It's a grand feeling to belong. No one wants to feel apart from. Kids relate to one another. They pick each other up when one falls. They tell secrets and laugh and cry together. They often feel more comfortable and loved by peers than they do by their families. And they feel more understood.

Peer pressure comes in many forms and can actually be good for all involved. Kids need friends. We all need friends. Sometimes it happens that a young person will become involved in a group that isn't exactly the most honest or safest group to belong to. When a situation of drug use comes up, it makes it difficult to decline the invitation and not feel inadequate. Instead of leaving the situation and risk the loss of face or friends, a person more than likely will give in against their better judgment. Not all kids, though. Those with good refusal skills will turn down a dangerous offer with pride.

THE PUSH TOWARD DRUGS

These influences do more to push a young person toward the use of mood and mind altering chemicals than many of us want to believe. Parents who think they are doing the best they can to steer their kids away from the forces that offer drugs are, in effect, leading them straight to drugs. A young person's life is built on the impressions that they are exposed to. If we fill them up with trash, it's no wonder that some young lives look for something to take them out of the mess. Instead of learning to deal with life's ups and downs, they covertly are being taught to give up and find some other resource to save them. Those resources often happen to be drugs.

Better resources are available, and that's why I've decided to write this book. The best game is played with the best resources at hand. Your kid's drug-proofing team needs a valuable key player on his or her side. The more choices that are known and available, the easier it is to go on for the win.

III

WHAT TO DO IF YOU FIND OUT
THE WORST

E ven the best parenting skills that you have or
the special love that you give your kid does
not always guarantee that he or she will not use
or abuse a drug. Sometimes, it just happens. Especially
with the strong influences that I described in the chapter before this one.

Kids who are found to be using mind or mood altering substances can still become drug-free. You can continue being a key player on their drug-proofing team.
At this point the game becomes more competitive and
the strategy changes. Don't give up now—the playing
field still has room for you. The game isn't won yet.
There's plenty of time to raise the score in your team's
favor.

LIGHTS...

Let's imagine that your worst fears are confirmed. It
has now become evident that your child has been using

a certain drug or various drugs. This is where those uncomfortable feelings of fear and hopelessness come in. You may experience shame. And you may become angry. All in all, it's sometimes a complete feeling of powerlessness. But, whether you know it or not, you do have control and power over the situation. All is not lost. There still is hope. Some parents on learning the worst, don't know whether to feel enraged or relieved that they finally have found the reason for their children's inappropriate behaviors. It is not unusual to experience hurt and pain. After all, this is your child. This is the little person that you have raised with the belief that they would be safe from the evils of drugs.

CAMERA...

Try not to overreact. Panic has a tendency to cause problems to escalate and grow bigger. To ignore the problem for fear of how to handle it won't make it go away. There are solutions to dealing with drug using situations. Any mistakes in handling this discovery can be kept to a minimum by **focusing on what you should not do**. These 'do nots' are outlined on the next page.

1. DON'T DENY THE OBVIOUS.

Chemical dependency or addiction is defined as a "disease of denial." Denial, not only of the one using the drugs, but of the parents or family as well. So often parents and other members under the same roof have a tendency to turn a deaf ear to the problem or look the other way and pretend that it doesn't exist. Telling yourself that, "It's probably not as bad as I think," or "It will go away on it's own in time," are fairly common statements that parents tell themselves. Thinking this way comes from being in shock over finding out the worst. This isn't the time to rationalize the 'why' or to minimize the scope of the problem. Now is the time to move forward and accept the fact that this is really happening. Denial at this stage only further allows dependency to advance to a more severe degree.

2. DON'T BLAME YOURSELF.

Switching gears and going into the 'self-pity' mode will only cause any further efforts to become stifled. All the blame in the world is not going to change what has already happened. It is not going to cause you to wake up from a bad dream. The key player who feels sorry for his or herself is at a major disadvantage for scoring the points needed to win the game.

Remember, chemical dependency is brought on by several different factors. Those addicted are responsible for their own actions. A good expression to keep in mind is that, "We are responsible to our children, not for our children."

3. DON'T BLAME OTHERS

Pointing the finger at other people or situations will do absolutely nothing to help the problem. There are those who compulsively choose to do a 'Geographical escape'. They rationalize that by moving to another street address or even out of town, the problem will be resolved. This does sound like an almost logical and magical cure, but it isn't. Their thinking is that the influences and unsafe conditions will cease to affect their kids if they are placed in different surroundings. The sad fact is that there are drugs and drug using people in every element of society. Unless someone chooses to live in a cave or on a mountain, they need to be prepared for the reality of drug use in America—in virtually every city.

A geographical escape may help for awhile, but this is only a short term solution. It's a matter of 'bandaiding' the problem. And if you have a child who is chemically dependent, the illness lies within them, not outside. Dependency will follow them wherever they make their home. Unless, of course, they receive help for their dependency, and are clean and sober in a program of recovery.

4. DON'T ENABLE

Enabling is to either consciously or unconsciously support a drug user's behavior. It is done by protecting the one with the abuse or addiction problem from taking responsibility for his/her own actions.

Parents who enable sometimes allow the person caught abusing drugs to promise that "It won't happen again." Or they bail them out of juvenile detention over and over again. Another way that parents enable is by making excuses or taking the blame themselves for their kid's drug induced problems. I will admit that it is tough not to enable. As parents, we often feel that it is our responsibility to save our children from any and all consequences that would cause them pain or heartbreak. This is a good rule to follow, generally speaking, but when it deals with behaviors brought on by mind and mood altering chemicals, it is a bad rule to follow.

I don't want to say that we should stand back and watch our child go down the tubes. Anyone addicted to drugs should get help for this problem. Anytime that someone's life is at risk, the problem needs to be dealt with immediately. But to enable behaviors such as crimes, poor attitudes, or irresponsible decisions is to silently say "It's okay to continue with what you are doing. We'll take care of the problems that you are creating." Not only is this extremely stressful for parents to do, but it fails to address and rectify the core issue.

ACTION ...

Now is the time to confront your child and inform him or her of what you see, know, and are concerned about. This stage usually sends jitters up and down a parent's spine. But a good key player has emotional control.

Be prepared first, to hear some rationalizing, "But mom, I smoke this to relax." Some justifying, "All the other kids do this, so what's the big deal?" And denying, "This isn't mine. I'm holding it for a friend." Don't be surprised if you also hear an admission such as, "Yeah, you're right. This is mine. I think that I might have a slight problem with it." Make absolutely certain that you have all of your facts straight before confronting. Write them down on paper if you have to. This is a very important step to take. It not only gets the possibility of a problem out into the open, but it relieves the pressure on yourself of what to do about it. Now you do know what to do about it. In order not to mess this whole process up, let's look at what to do next and what not to do.

1. DON'T USE GUILT

"Do you have any idea how much you have hurt us?" Or, "How could you do such a thing?" These statements will only serve to raise the defenses of a child. Especially when they are already caught in an uncomfortable position. Using guilt tends to create a hostile and angry situation, and should be avoided at all costs. Remember this when confronting: **Hate the illness—love the child.** If your kid is caught up in the grasp of addiction, he or she is dumbfounded as to how to get out of it. Try not to make matters worse with guilt statements.

2. STAY CALM

I know that this sounds easier than it really is. Getting angry will only create a small war between you and your kid and you both will lose. There are rarely winners in wars. Name calling or bringing up past issues is out, also. A situation that turns ugly will only tend to give a child more of an unrealistic reason to continue to use drugs.

Showing concern and unconditional love are the most powerful weapons to use. They keep the situation from turning into a battleground. If you must, take several deep breaths before confronting. Speak in a slow, calm, and easy-to-understand voice. If you find your child

STAY CALM

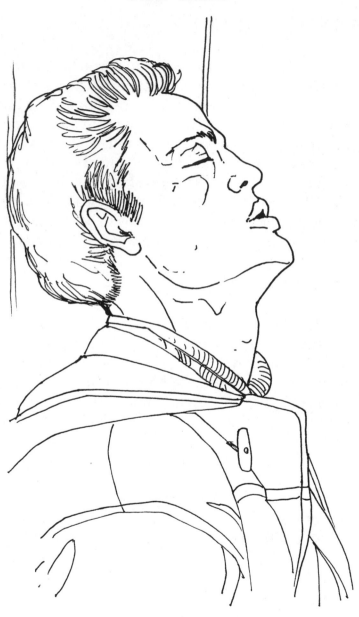

getting defensive and shouting, continue to stay calm and repeat your concerns. You may have to discontinue the conversation until things cool down and then try again.

3. DON'T USE SHAME

Shame is an ugly tool to have in your arsenal. Saying things like, "Look what you're doing to yourself," or "I hope you feel terrible about this", does no good. A drug using kid usually has no idea what they are doing to themselves. Shame is often felt by the parents, and it's an almost unconscious vengeance to make the other person feel the same way. It's the old "If I'm going to feel this bad —then you are too."

4. STATE YOUR CONCERNS

Now comes the moment of truth. This is the part that we parents dread the most. Remember, not only are you on your kid's team, but you are the key player. This means that you have the most experience and logic needed to win this game. Backing down at this point only gives the other team the advantage. This is the moment where points count in winning the game.

Express your concerns to your child. Tell the child what you know or suspect and let him/her know that it needs to be discussed. Mirror back to your child the behaviors and attitudes that you have observed and present any evidence that has been gathered.

Let him or her know that you are concerned and want to help. Make it plain that you will do everything in your power to see that this problem is looked at and dealt with.

. Be prepared for the unexpected. You may hear responses of sarcasm, anger, denial, or a lack of understanding of what it is you are concerned about. Common sense and showing interest in getting to the bottom of this will go a long way. Don't back down at this point. Remember, backing down is enabling behavior on your part. Keep in mind that this problem will not go away on it's own. And that you may be doing more harm by abandoning the situation than by facing it and dealing with it.

THE NEXT STEP...

A key player uses resources offered by others in building strength for a game well won. A phone call to a local drug and alcohol treatment facility, mental health center, or physician is the next step. This in no way takes away your position in the game. It serves only to get clarification as to whether your kid really has a problem or not. It's better to be safe than sorry.

Those professionals versed in chemical dependency will be able to pin down the problem in no time. If there is a problem.

When the day of the appointment comes, an evaluation or assessment will be performed on the one with the possible problem. It usually involves a person filling out an intake form asking for basic personal information. This is followed by different diagnostic tests on paper. These are normally true and false questions that deal with drug using behaviors and drug types and usage. Parents are often asked to also fill out a questionnaire. This collateral information is also used in determining whether there is a problem or not. It asks about the behaviors and attitudes that you have observed in your child. Also, some of the questions inquire into whether you have direct evidence of a possible drug problem and to list them if you do. After the diagnostic testing is finished, your child will then sit down with a clinician, who will ask a series of questions dealing with signs and symptoms that could point to a possible problem with drugs.

Don't worry that your child may be somewhat angry about this entire process and therefore less than honest. Certain 'control' questions are built into the tests and personal interview questions. These questions are actually 'trick' questions and can only be answered one way. They are used to tell whether a person being evaluated understands them, if they are in denial, or are telling lies. An example of a control question may be, "Is there anyone at your school that you do not like?" Regardless of how friendly and outgoing a child is, it's pretty rare that they would like everybody at their school.

The clinician at the completion of the evaluation, puts the answers from the diagnostic tests, the collateral information, and the interview answers together and looks for a pattern of signs and symptoms. This takes detective-like work by a skilled professional who knows what to look for. After perusing the answers, the clinician can then make a determination of a correct diagnosis. It is possible for a drug abusing kid to scam the system and beat the clinician at his own game. This has happened to the best of professionals. Especially if the person being evaluated is 'treatment wise.' This term applies to someone who may have been through this process before or even in treatment at one time or more in the past. They may have learned the ins and outs and know the answers that will show that there isn't a problem when there is. The ones that scam the process are in the minority though. When I evaluate a youngster, I pay special attention to the words they use and the terms that are conveyed. This can usually tip me off that they are treatment wise. But no one is perfect and one or two may be able to slip through the cracks once in a great while. Sometimes a simple test such as a urinalysis will tell the truth and nothing but the truth. Especially on a kid who denies any drug use, but then comes up positive for marijuana, amphetamines, or such. Thank goodness for this method. It's an old standby. Some kids will even admit to using chemicals after being asked for a urine sample, just to save themselves the trouble and embarrassment of looking silly when it comes back dirty.

How do you get a kid to accompany you to an office for an evaluation if he or she refuses to go? Some parents use the reward system, such as promising a meal or item afterwards. Some use the threat of consequences for not complying with their requests. I often tell parents of resistant kids to convince them to prove that mom and dad are wrong. To go for the evaluation and show that they don't have a problem. Kids love to prove us wrong sometimes. Especially if they are angry at the accusations of drug use.

What if they still refuse to budge and are adamant about not leaving the house? That's not unusual in many adolescents. Especially if they have a definite drug problem and are into denial. The next best step is to contact your child's school and alert a counselor to the problem. Most schools, today, have what are called 'intervention specialists.' These are trained drug prevention counselors who assist students in getting help for possible drug problems. They can be an asset when a kid plants his or her heels in the ground and refuses to budge. Don't be ashamed about talking to school officials about the possibility of your kid having a drug problem. You just may save his or her life.

THE VERDICT

Once a child is evaluated and the results are complete, it becomes time for the verdict. The clinician who did the original evaluation will sit down with you and the young person and explain the results. This moment of truth brings a rush of anxiety to parents. "Does my child not have a problem?" "Could this all be a misunderstanding?" "Is my kid an addict? And if so, what's next?" These are typical questions that we all ask ourselves before the verdict is read.

There are four levels that are used to show where a person is, in relation to using a drug or drugs. A young person who is at any one of the first three levels is not considered chemically dependent. I don't want to convey that these three levels show the lack of a problem. Any drug use by young people should be considered a problem. Continued use of chemicals beyond an evaluation can turn into full blown addiction at anytime in the future.

The four levels, in order of severity, are:

1. Use
2. Misuse
3. Abuse
4. Addiction

1. USE

This is experimental use of drugs. Maybe they have been tried one or two times out of curiosity or pressure from peers. There are usually no problems that have materialized out of the use of drugs at this level.

2. MISUSE

Shows that the person is using drugs on a somewhat regular basis. Some minor problems may be felt as a result of drug use.

3. ABUSE

Preoccupation has set in. This person thinks and plans for their next drug use on an almost daily basis. Hiding and sneaking drugs and the use of them is common. The person begins to rebel slightly against school and family rules. Personal values and goals begin to diminish. A change in attitude and behavior is noticeable. Legal problems can set in at this level.

4. ADDICTION

This shows compulsive use of drugs. The person at this point has lost control over their drug use. It becomes

an obsession and a priority over other needs. It becomes
difficult to quit. Health problems may become noticeable. Mental confusion can set in. A drastic change in
behavior and attitude is seen. Legal problems can become more prevalent.

Knowing that a child is at any of these levels is reason to be concerned. But don't feel that nothing can be
done to rectify the problem—it can. The game isn't over
until it's over! And you're still the key player holding
the prime moves.

I have seen many different reactions by parents when
I inform them of the verdict. Some cry. Others show
anger. Relief is seen on some faces. And then there are
those that are shocked and almost appear to be coma-
tose. I have yet to see a parent be overjoyed and happy
that their kid has a problem. And I hope never to.

Not all kids show a problem. Some will be evaluated
as NSP or having "No Significant Problem." These are
the one's that may have been able to scam the clinician
on the evaluation. And maybe they really don't have a
problem. Sometimes, parents make a mistake in their
suspicions. But as I said earlier, it is better to be safe
than sorry. If this becomes the case, at least it will be
great comfort to know that they don't have a problem.

Being at any of these levels shows the person to be
definitely using drugs. This is reason to be concerned.
The clinician will then make a recommendation for the
person evaluated to receive some type of help or

assistance for their drug problem. Education alone may be what is needed for some at the use and misuse levels. This will give them the facts needed to see what drugs can do to them in the long run. It can show them that the decision to put chemicals into one's body is a poor choice. Others at the more intense levels will need some type of therapy or treatment. These are well structured programs to meet their needs and to get them off drugs and on the road to recovery.

It always amazes me to hear parents say, "We'll think about it, and get back to you." And more times than I can remember, they don't. What happens? I suppose that once they leave my office, they decide that the problem will go away on it's own. Maybe, the person evaluated with a drug problem promises to never do drugs again. Or some parents probably just deny that the problem exists. They may choose instead to forget that this entire scenario ever took place. Sad to say, I've never seen the problem go away without some type of help, support, or treatment for someone with a significant problem with drugs. This is especially true for a person who is diagnosed with addiction or dependency.

WHAT MAKES DEPENDENCY/ ADDICTION A DISEASE?

Chemical dependency or what can also be called addiction is defined as a disease. We're not talking about something as petty as the common cold. We're talking about an illness that can and does end lives. And at times, rather quickly. Especially among the young. Addiction has the same criteria used to describe a disease.

It's primary—This is to say that it is not caused by another disorder. It is, in itself, the cause of other disorders. Addiction is first in importance.

It's progressive—If left untreated, it will only get worse. Continued use of mood and mind altering substances will cause it to go from a mild stage to a more severe stage.

It's multifaceted—It influences all areas of a person's life in a harmful and detrimental way. This includes physical, mental, and spiritual areas.

It's chronic—Meaning that it is permanent and ongoing. Once drug use is stopped, the disease is in remission. The person diagnosed with a chronic disease will always have it. A return to drugs after stopping them for any length of time, brings it out of remission and into activity.

It's fatal—Continued use of any type of mood and mind altering substance can lead to death. Fatalities can be caused by numerous factors, such as: Liver disease, auto accidents, suicides, etc.

It's prevalent—It is a common disease. The United States is known to have the highest rate of addiction in the world.

It's treatable—With a structured course of action, it can be arrested.

Being chemically dependent is not the end of the world. The last criteria listed above shows this—it is treatable. Abstinence, therapy, support, and faith in one's own ability can place a chemically dependent person back on the course to a sober and positive lifestyle.

In order to get young persons back on track with their life, it's mandatory to first get them sober. This is where treatment or therapy comes in. A person who is resistant to an evaluation may be extremely resistant to of changing his or her life. Or, as I prefer to say, 'saving their life." And others that willfully sit down for an evaluation, especially if they deny a definite problem, may also balk at the idea of treatment. This is to be expected. I don't know too many people who are thrilled to death about getting help for a problem that they deny even exists. And then there are some kids who will jump at the chance to get help. They have recognized that the use of chemicals has disrupted their lives and they wAnt to make a change. Treatment today, is a whole lot different than it was in years past. Now it is geared and structured for each individual. What is looked at is a person's attitudes, behaviors, emotional and physical well-being, and other important factors that are taken into consideration in order to create a plan of action. This plan of action is specifically structured for each person. It is much more efficient than the old way of doing things, which was one type of plan for everyone—period.

There are different types of treatment programs that are available for a chemically dependent young person. The clinician who performed the initial evaluation will recommend what type of program is best suited for the individual with the addiction problem.

The next chapter will explain these different treatment programs, and what to look for in making sure your child gets the best possible help available if he or she needs it. We'll look at what recovery is, as well as other important-to-know information that is indispensable to a key player.

IV

CHANGING THE WORST INTO THE BEST

M aking the transition from active addiction to living without the use of drugs is not the easiest task to fulfill. This is especially true for an adolescent. First of all, recovery from all mood and mind altering substances takes breaking through any denial that may exist. This will be the central focus in treatment for a child who fails to see that drugs have had a profound negative effect on his or her life. Those not in denial will first be taught how to accept the illness that they have. All in all, the person in treatment will be shown how to make healthy decisions, use support and other empowering tools for healthy, positive growth.

Recovery from chemicals is not just about being clean and sober. It's more than that. It's about changing old behaviors, attitudes, and ways of thinking. Recovery means giving up the old life and exchanging it for a new one. It reminds me of most fairy tales that end, "And they lived happily ever after." And most do, if they follow what they have learned in a drug treatment facility. Sure, life still puts little roadblocks in the paths of young people. But they will learn how to get beyond them without the use of mood or mind altering chemicals.

There are different types of treatment available. The clinician who performed the evaluation and recommended treatment will clarify which type of treatment the person with the drug problem needs. Let's look at the various types that are out there.

OUTPATIENT TREATMENT

Outpatient treatment provides a structured plan using individual and group counseling. Some programs have a family component built in, where family members and patients will attend together once every week or two. This is essential in any type of treatment for young people. Family involvement is a must. This rings true for any and all treatment programs. There are many treatment centers who will refuse to admit a patient unless the family is committed to attending family groups.

Admission to this type of program usually means that the patient is expected to attend anywhere from a few months to a couple of years. Sessions are normally held in the afternoon or evenings to accommodate those going to school or working. Since this type of program allows a person to attend only a certain number of hours a day or week, random urinalysis tests are given.

People who are at a low risk to relapse or are at an early stage of addiction are amenable to this type of program. Also, since this kind of treatment is lower priced than any of the others, it makes it simpler for those who are strapped for funds. Some treatment centers will require those at risk to relapse, to sign a contract committing to agree to a higher level of care (such as inpatient treatment) if they can not stay clean and sober. Resistant kids who refuse to cooperate in group process or are too unruly or inappropriate get very little out of outpatient treatment. They are commonly discharged or referred to a more intense program.

This level of treatment is also recommended to young people who are users, misusers, or abusers. Of course these people do the best, as their drug problem is less severe than those addicted. Assignments are often given to patients to take home and complete, and to bring back to share with the counselor and/or the entire group. Patients are also expected to attend support groups outside of group therapy on their own time. I'll discuss support groups later in this chapter. Treatment may help a person to stay drug-free, but they need support outside of the therapy setting, too.

DAY TREATMENT

Day treatment is slightly more intense than regular outpatient treatment. The patient spends the better part of each day in this kind of program. Typically from early morning to late afternoon. The patient is then allowed to go home after each daily session is finished. Most programs run a full five days a week.

This type of program is designed for those who are not at risk of relapsing while going through treatment for their drug problems. Some people are transitioned to day treatment after completing inpatient treatment.

INPATIENT TREATMENT

These programs offer a controlled, highly structured, safe, and supported environment. Patients are housed in a hospital-like setting, 24 hours a day. The schedule from early morning to evening is intensive and strict. Most facilities that offer this type of program have medical staff available to monitor those patients who are experiencing withdrawal symptoms that could be life threatening. Other facilities have psychiatrists on board to work with patients diagnosed with other problems than addiction, such as emotional disorders. Treatment is offered in group settings and individually. This type of program keeps the patient in a secure environment, eliminating any outside influences that could cause a patient to relapse.

Kids have been known to 'escape' from such treatment centers. Unless of course they are admitted to what are known as 'lock down' facilities. That means that the doors are secured and locked. It is not possible for someone to walk out or run away. Kids that are resistant to inpatient treatment and are at risk to run away are usually referred to this type of facility. Most programs of this type vary anywhere from a couple of weeks to well over a month. The cost is substantially higher than outpatient treatment.

RESIDENTIAL TREATMENT

This is a supervised, 24 hour a day program where the patient lives in a staffed facility for anywhere from a couple of months to over a year. This type of program is for the person who is at the greatest risk to relapse. Most patients admitted to residential treatment have exhausted other types of treatment with little or no change in their drug using behaviors. A program of this kind is a last resort for many drug using kids.

HALFWAY HOUSES

This type of program is designed to be a temporary living situation once a person has been discharged from inpatient treatment. It provides more intense structure and support than an outpatient program would. Those at a high risk of relapsing due to peer pressures or family dysfunction are placed here to learn more about the 'essentials of recovery.'

Halfway houses provide treatment for an average of three to six months. They are less intense and more short term than residential treatment.

SHOPPING FOR SOBRIETY

It's important to find out what any program offers before admitting a young person into it. Each facility that offers services has their own standards and mode of care that they carry out to help kids who are chemically dependent. Don't think for a minute that they all offer the same thing—they don't. Like any service available, there are good ones and there are bad ones. Before giving the go ahead for your kid to enter any kind of program, check each one out first. Find out what services it provides and what it's success rate is.

- Are staff counselors certified or licensed?

- Is some type of recreational therapy offered?

- How long has the program been in existence?

- Is it mandatory for patients to attend twelve-step support groups such as Alcoholics Anonymous?

- What type of therapy is offered?

- Does it have a family program?

- What is the policy if a child runs away?

- Are decision-making skills taught?

- Is the program tailored to each patient's specific needs?

- Does it provide a safe and secure environment?

Finding out the cost of the program is also important. Each treatment facility has different rates and payment plans. Also, some insurance companies will pay benefits to one and not to another. Make sure to find the answers to these questions before going ahead and admitting your kid into any type of program. The cost of treatment is not cheap. Although, in the long run, it could save your child's life. Consider it an investment in his or her future.

Insurance companies are tightening the reins on treatment for individuals. Managed Care companies are more apt to pay for less intense treatment than what is recommended by the evaluating clinician. Unless you feel comfortable making payments on treatment costs that your insurance coverage doesn't meet, you may have to settle for a lower level of care. This is better than no care at all.

Any program that deals with addiction in kids or adults needs to be well-structured and offer more than just getting people off of drugs. It should deal with other issues as well. Refusal skills, reaching out for support, enhancing self-esteem, anger management, proper exercise, and healthy eating habits are just a few. You may even want to ask what they do to break through an individual's denial system. As I have mentioned earlier, this should be the central focus of any program.

WHY DENY THE OBVIOUS?

As I promised earlier, I will explain what denial is and the importance of breaking through it.

Just why would someone diagnosed with a serious illness deny this very fact? Especially after being evaluated and shown point blank that they have it. What makes a person continue to risk his or her life with the knowledge that death waits just around the corner? What could cause someone to refuse needed medical help?

The answer is simple. Denial. Denial is the mind's safety zone. It's used in order to protect a person from having to look at or face a dreadful situation. It's a safe haven from having to deal with fear, pain, or hurt. Denial isn't just manifested in drug using individuals. It's seen in people with other illnesses, such as diabetes, cancer, etc. And it does not just plague those with illnesses. People in abusive or dysfunctional relationships also tend to deny that there is a problem. It's also common in someone who may lose somebody close to them due to death. It's the old "What I don't see or know won't hurt me" syndrome. And it affects millions of different people in different situations every day.

A patient diagnosed with diabetes may feel embarrassed or shameful at having this illness.

A patient diagnosed with cancer may feel fear about chemotherapy or other treatment.

A patient diagnosed with a drug problem may feel uncomfortable about giving up chemicals that gain relief from emotional pain.

What the three patients have in common are illnesses that are difficult to accept. Especially when they involve making changes or accepting help in order to lengthen their lives.

SHORT LIVED SELF-DECEPTION

Denial is usually an unconscious act and is effective in letting one not see the problem that exists in his/her life. This does sound comfortable and effective in not having to deal with the bad side of life. But the truth is that denial is short lived. This means that it only works for a short time and can be and usually is catastrophic in the long run. The situation, whether it is an illness or a hopeless relationship tends to progress further into a more severe and possibly life threatening condition. The three illnesses listed above are all prone to advance to a more serious stage.

THE CURE FOR DENIAL

Learning all you can about whatever ails you is the first step in breaking through denial. Looking at the personal problems that surround you and linking them with the primary cause is the second. Listening to others with the same illness or situation and speaking openly about your own is also paramount to coming to acceptance. Acceptance is admitting to having a problem in one's life. It's learning that in spite of having an illness or being in a seemingly lose-lose situation, it can be changed. Acceptance is not about agreeing with or welcoming whatever it is that troubles you, but a means of coming to terms with the choices available to correct it. And last but not least it's a commitment to accept help for one's problem.

In drug treatment facilities, denial is looked at and spoken to at the beginning of any therapy. Most programs have their patients write out an autobiography. Special emphasis is placed on type of drugs used, frequency of use, quantities used, reasons for use, what was expected from the use, consequences of use, and the negative effects that drug use had on the person ingesting them as well as others such as friends and family.

It's hard to deny having a problem when you have it written down in front of you in black and white. Most people coming out of denial are amazed at how severe their problem really is. These autobiographies are usually read out loud in group. This lets the young person with the problem get it out into the open and eliminates it from being a 'big secret.' Once this is done, most patients are more open-minded and more willing to participate in treatment and make the changes necessary to live a drug-free life.

MIRACLES AND BENEFITS OF RECOVERY

Living a 'program' free from the use of mood and mind altering substances isn't only about not using these substances. It's about a new way of life. It's about living life to it's fullest and getting the most out of it. I have seen people who work hard at living a drug-free life become better capable of contributing to this world than those without a problem with drugs. Recovering people seem to take life more seriously and to have more strength to overcome insurmountable odds. These are some of the miracles and benefits that people in recovery receive:

- The knowledge of healthy choices and the freedom to choose.

- The ability to love oneself, others, and to feel loved by others.

- Increased faith and an open and honest relationship with a greater power.

- Freedom from unfounded fears of people, changes, places, and situations.

- The ability to appreciate nature, art, music, religion, etc.

- Freedom to attain and to nourish healthy relationships.

- The gift of being honest with oneself and others.

- Peace of mind and confidence.

- Enjoyment of fellowship with family, friends, and others.

- The realization of and respect for equality among all people.

- The gift of forgiveness.

- The ability to make amends to those harmed.

- Compassion.

- The gift of prayer.

- Freedom from the bondage of the past.

Who could ask for more than this? It almost sounds like a dream that could not possibly come true. But it is real. I've had the pleasure of seeing it become reality in the lives of countless kids. But this is only if they continue to stay clean and sober and live a program that includes attending support groups. The disease of addiction doesn't go away after a certain amount of time. People in recovery have to continue to be aware of their disease and to abide by what they learned in treatment. They must never forget where they came from, and the way it was when they were caught in the web of active addiction.

Drug treatment gets a person clean and sober, makes them aware of the problem, and then gives them the tools to walk the path of sobriety after they discharge from the program. After leaving treatment, there are things that are important for them to continue to do. Recovering children learn throughout their treatment program to take personal responsibility for their own recovery.

DISCHARGING FROM TREATMENT

There are several things that the key players also need to be aware of and apply in their **own** lives after a child leaves a drug program. I have listed them here.

1. SEEK GUIDANCE FOR YOURSELF

Since chemical dependency affects family members as well as the one dependent, it is wise to seek outside support and help. There often are many unresolved issues when a child returns from treatment. There may still be resentments, anger, shame, and a host of other feelings that need to be dealt with.

Support groups such as Al-Anon or Families Anonymous are excellent resources. You'll meet and be involved with other parents and family members who are going through the same experience as you are. These meetings will give you a 'safe place' to talk openly and honestly about the way you feel and the concerns that you may have. You'll also be able to express the joys and triumphs that you have over seeing your child getting healthier. The meeting places and times can be found by calling the phone numbers listed in the phone book.

2. HAVE PATIENCE

It wasn't overnight that your child developed a drug problem, so everything's not going to be solved overnight. A kid coming out of treatment is still a kid. He or she is still going to behave in ways you wished they didn't. There are going to be times when discipline is appropriate. Their attitudes and behaviors may swing left and right. Have patience. I'm not saying to treat them differently than before. Children still need to be responsible and follow the family rules. Being chemically dependent does not give anyone the right to be above or better treated than others.

Keep in mind that sobriety is a whole different ballgame to them, especially if they have been involved with drugs for quite some time. The transition back into society without drugs to fall back on can be uneasy and tense.

3. BE THERE FOR THEM

Supporting a young person fresh out of treatment is crucial. They may be going through all kinds of confusing and uncomfortable adjustments. Give them room to change. Let them know that you are there for them. Give them praise and encouragement when you see that they are staying clean and sober. Help them get involved in activities or hobbies.

It's very difficult for most parents to let their children out of the house after they are discharged from a drug program.

There is still that fear that they may go out and resume the use of drugs. This is a logical concern. It is impossible to watch them 24 hours a day. If a person really wants to do drugs, they're going to do them—regardless how strict or controlling the parents are. Trust has to be earned. Teach this to them. Let them earn it back little by little, by proving that they can make the right choices.

4. KEEP COMMUNICATION OPEN

Communicating with your child is, of course, important. So is communicating with their school, their counselor, other family members, friends, and their friend's parents. Discuss with these other confidantes any concerns you have or problems that you may see your child experiencing. Don't feel that you have to do this alone — you don't.

A kid coming home from treatment makes for a trying time for parents. It can also be a trying time for the one returning. Everything will not be perfect all of the time. I can assure you of this. Be careful not to set expectations on his or her recovery. This tends to set you up for a fall when these expectations fail to materialize. Just be grateful and thankful that this young person in your life has been given a second chance at living a productive life. Never take their treatment or recovery for granted.

STANDING IN THE SHOES OF THOSE IN RECOVERY

Put yourself in the place of a kid returning home from a drug treatment center. It's helpful to use some empathy and try and see through their eyes what it's like to 'start over again.' Recovering kids usually feel:

APPREHENSIVE

Someone once described the feeling of early recovery as crawling on your hands and knees backwards on a sheet of glass. This is like a new life for anyone giving up drugs. It's hard for them to know what to expect next.

TENSE

What will I do if drugs are offered to me? How will I change my old friends? What if my parents accuse me

APPREHENSIVE

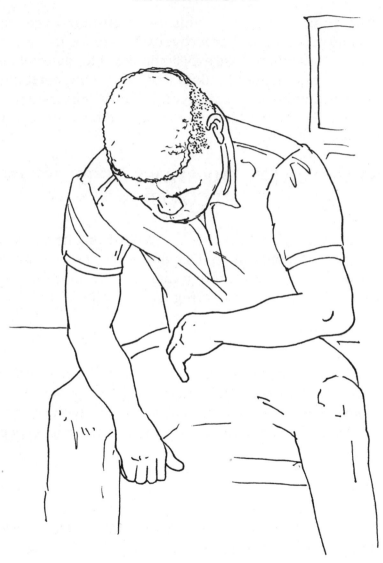

of using drugs when I haven't? These are legitimate concerns. The more recovery a person has, the more confident they will become in themselves.

BOREDOM

Since most of a recovering kid's activities were formerly centered around drug using activities, he or she will feel an emptiness that will need to be filled. Finding drug-free friends, places, and things to do will eliminate boredom from his/her life.

GUILT

Being back home after treatment and remembering the problems that they caused before giving up drugs, will bring on guilt. A young person in recovery may feel the need to talk about this and to possibly make amends to those harmed. It is important to listen to what they have to say.

THE TRANSITION BACK TO SCHOOL

Students returning to school after beginning recovery are usually terrified. They fear rejection by their peers and the possibility of academic failure. School employees do a good job in prevention efforts, intervention, and referrals for help. What is even more important is how they deal with a returning student who is in recovery. It may be a good idea to share this list of teacher "Do's and Don'ts," so as to better assist any kid who may be transitioning back.

TEACHER DO'S

- Be flexible but consistent.

- Tell the young person you understand where they have been. Encourage him/her to stay clean and sober.

- Tell students that they can talk to you privately if they feel the need to.

- Make them aware that they are using their recovery as an excuse to avoid responsibility, if you notice they are.

TEACHER DON'TS

- Don't feel sorry for, or pity, recovering students.

- Don't avoid them.

- Don't use their past as a weapon against them.

• Don't allow them to do less than others because they are in recovery.

RECOVERY SUPPORT GROUPS

People in recovery from addiction to drugs need to attend support groups. This is a must. The chances of them going back out and getting involved in drugs again, is lessened considerably by attendance. The two support groups that are most recommended are Narcotics Anonymous and Alcoholics Anonymous.

They are both frequented by members who are dependent on drugs. Alcoholics Anonymous focuses primarily on those addicted to alcohol more so than other drugs. There is no charge to belong, as they are self-supporting through member's contributions. Meeting places and times can be found by calling the numbers listed in your phone book.

It's normal for anyone going to their first, second, or third support meeting to be nervous and anxious. Some cities have meetings that are made up entirely of young people. These two support groups that I mentioned, follow almost exactly the same twelve steps. These steps are basically 'guidelines' for living. They are the principles by which these groups are founded. Following these guidelines have changed more people's lives than I can count. They are part of the 'program' that recovering people need and use to live a life free from drugs.

And there is no doubt in my mind that they work. Each group also has a text that can be purchased and read to explain the program and the steps. It is a valuable tool for anyone in recovery.

Twelve step support groups need to be a priority over anything else in a young person's life. When he/she starts attending, the youth will be directed to obtain a sponsor. This is someone who has a quality amount of 'clean time' that can teach and guide the new member on the road to recovery. They are vitally important as a sounding board or for guidance when someone feels the urge to go back to the use of drugs. Being in recovery does not take away the influences that became a big part of a drug user's life before quitting drugs. Support groups can be of help in avoiding and dealing with some of the old influences.

One of the most important slogans to be learned in any twelve step support group is "One day at a time." This means that just for today, the person recovering will not use chemicals. Being aware of living life one day at a time takes the fear out of 'future tripping,' or looking down the road past today. It is accepting the fact that no one has the power to change what happened yesterday or to foretell tomorrow. Recovery is a "just for today" program.

A LOOK AT RELAPSE

A relapse occurs when someone who is in recovery makes a conscious choice to use drugs again, and then follows through with this choice. Young people in recovery have a much higher relapse rate than adults do. This has to do with the influences that I discussed earlier. A relapse can bring heavy feelings of guilt, remorse, and shame to a recovering person. It can also put the family situation into a dangerous tailspin. It can almost be as though starting from the beginning again. But it doesn't have to be. Some parents go back into the denial mode and pretend it didn't happen. Those with the addiction revert back to their old behaviors and attitudes. Even after a relapse, there still is hope.

Some kids will admit to going back to their old ways and stop on their own with the help of their support group. Some will need to re-enter a drug program in a more intense form to stay clean and sober. Relapses do happen to the best of recovering people. It is important for them to recognize what it was that caused them to relapse and to avoid the problem or situation in the future. Maybe the person wasn't living the program to it's potential and needs to attend more support groups or obtain a sponsor. Most people who relapse need to increase what they were doing when they were staying clean and sober.

Having a child who refuses, or is unable, to lay off drugs after being in recovery and continues to relapse numerous times is frightening. This is where the parents or the key player on their drug-proofing team needs to get tough. Consequences should be handed down immediately. This is not the time to back away from the situation. Doing this only serves to place everybody back to square one. Some parents give their children an ultimatum, to cease doing drugs or leave. This may sound drastic, but the fear of having to leave one's home may be enough to work. And if it doesn't work—follow through. Threats mean nothing to kids unless they are carried out. This shows that you mean business. It shows that you will not tolerate drug use in your home. It also shows that you love your child and do not want to see them die.

Writing up a contract is also a good tool to use. If a child agrees to give up using drugs and to continue in a recovery program, put it in writing. Stipulate what is expected of them and what the consequences are if the contract is violated. Follow through swiftly if the terms of the contract are not met.

You can play an important part as a key player in looking for and recognizing certain signs of impending relapse in a recovering child. Once noticed, discuss with him or her what you have recognized and ask what you can do to help. Almost all treatment centers teach the recognition of relapse symptoms.

If noticed early enough, it can head off a potential disaster.

RELAPSE WARNING SIGNS

Insomnia

Impulsive or compulsive behavior

Isolation or loneliness

Unresolved or intense anger

Resentments

Discontinuance of support groups

Periods of confusion

Depression

Difficulty in the management of stress

Defensiveness

Irregular eating habits

Lack of motivation

INSOMNIA

Self pity

Dishonesty

Shame or guilt

Intense frustration

Worrying more about others than self

Difficulty in expressing feelings

Association with drug using peers

Denial of addiction

Loss of self confidence

Giving up of goals and aspirations

Urges to use drugs

Health problems

Dissatisfaction with life

THE ROAD AHEAD

Recovery from the use of drugs is a lifetime commitment. Nobody graduates from recovery. A cure for addiction is nowhere in sight. With continued support and
care, you as a key player can continue to play an important role on your kid's drug-proofing team. The game
continues on, and the best game is the one that has a
team with the most efficient strategies. Even in recovery, the part that you play on your kid's team is to continue to help him/her maintain a drug-free life. There
are many examples of young people coming back to
score big points and to lead the game. Stand by your
child. Out of all the tools that a kid possesses to stay
clean and sober, one of the most important—is you.

V

STOPPING THE WORST BEFORE IT STARTS

I've always been an advocate of drug prevention efforts. It's always been easier to head off a potential drug problem than it is to get someone out of a drug problem. Television, on some shows, is informing young people about the evils of drug use. The printed media is getting the message out that people and drugs don't mix. Movies are showing far less glamorization of drug use than ever before. Schools are pushing "Just Say No" programs. Even the churches are getting involved in putting out the message that "Drugs can mess up a child's life." But what are the most influential people in a kid's life doing about it? Who are they, you ask? Parents! They're you and me and all others that have young children.

Recent surveys have shown that parents are still the most significant people in a kid's life today. These surveys were answered by our kids, not some adult sitting in front of a calculator, coming up with numbers to impress us and to make us feel loved. Kids today, claim that their mothers and fathers are the ones that they look up to the most. A lot has happened in the world in the last century. Lots of things have changed for the worse. It's nice to know that our sons and our daughters continue to look up to each of us.

Prevention efforts directed at children need to begin in the home. Most parents are uncomfortable with even the thought of bringing the subject up. Some parents have too little or no information themselves to discuss it. Others talk about it in either a threatening or a passive way. The big question is:

If we are the most important people in our kid's lives, shouldn't we learn all that we can and teach them? And the answer is:

Of course we should. That's what this chapter is all about. It's about stopping the worst before it starts. It's about caring enough about our children's future, that we're willing to be a key player on their drug-proofing team. Even if you have a child who has abused drugs in the past or is in recovery now from addiction, this chapter is still for you. Drug-proofing our children should start the minute they learn to understand what we are saying. I personally believe that it should continue until after they reach retirement age.

Most of these pages will contain valuable instructions that you may not have been aware of. Some of them are old time ideas that parents already know, but have forgotten to use. They're simple and direct. A key player should have no trouble at all taking them out onto the playing field. These instructions will win the game against childhood drug use. And they will continue to be a mighty influence in winning game after game—if they are exercised.

DAYS OF OLD

As I stated earlier, a lot has changed in the past century. The biggest changes have taken place just within the last 60 years. The 1930's saw most families making their homes in small and close communities. A large percentage owned and operated their own farms. Sitting down for dinner together was the highlight of each day as family members shared their joys and sorrows. Everybody listened intensely and then reached out to support one another. Grandma and grandpa lived across the street and aunts and uncles down the block. They all upheld the family standards of good morals and values. It was a love they had for one another that bonded them together. There was no outside influence that could come between them. They were all one big happy family.

The family of today has changed considerably. Most live in the big cities. Mom and Dad both work and leave the house early to fight the traffic jams. After arriving home later that evening, they enter an empty house, as the children have eaten TV dinners and left for the mall.

Grandma and Grandpa live on the other side of the country and all the aunts and uncles are scattered from here to Europe. Each person in this household holds their own personal standards. Outside influences often come between family members. Television, rap music, negative peers, wild ideas, and self-centered attitudes have divided this family many times. Love still bonds them together—sometimes. And they usually are one big happy family. That is, when they are together as a family.

So you see, times have changed. They've changed in a short period of time, too. The family unit once was the core and central educating force that gave kids the essentials needed to live a safe life. Today, many families depend on schools, law enforcement, television, and a host of other influences to educate children on how to live safe lives. That's because most families are too busy doing their own thing. They become so occupied with keeping up with the rest of the world, that they fail to meet the needs of each other. What happens then is that the kids go elsewhere to get their needs met. They get them met by sitting in front of the boob tube for hours everyday. Listening to loud R-rated music that has little redeeming value. Talking on the phone until they develop cauliflower ear and hanging out with other kids who they feel understand them more than their own parents do. The family essentially disintegrates and fails to exist.

A family that communicates in healthy ways is a family that sticks together through thick and thin. It stays afloat when the rest of the world seems to be sinking. Problems that crop up out of nowhere are discussed openly and honestly and solved immediately. There's no beating around the bush before they are looked at. There's no ignoring them. A healthy family has it's share of problems, too. There's no getting around them sometimes. But they're dealt with in a democratic way.

Teaching a young person not to use drugs is more than telling them to "Just Say No." It involves more than describing different chemicals and the horrible effects that they have on those using them. To stop the worst before it starts means being there for your kids. Showing compassion, care, and love are vital ingredients. So are hope, faith, and trust. Being open-minded to learning new skills is another. Having healthy family skills is what this chapter is all about. Using what you read on these pages can do more than just create drug-free kids, they can build closeness and happiness in a family. Isn't that what a family should be all about? I believe so.

COMMUNICATION SAYS IT ALL

The most essential element of all drug prevention efforts is communication. Without proper and effective communication, the family tends to disintegrate.

Inconsistent behaviors on the part of the parents and the children are often seen and felt by everyone. The attitudes and actions of all who live under the same roof bring on chaos and turmoil. True communication is the heart of support, information, direction, and help. It is paramount in guiding young people through the potential problems associated with growing up. This includes the threat of drugs that have saturated our society. For some parents the thought of sitting down and talking to their kids is dreadful. For others it may appear simple, but there is sometimes that question of whether it is doing any good or not. For communication to be effective, it needs to be used over and over again. Not just once or twice a month. Regular communication between parents and kids needs to be incorporated into the family system for the results to be seen and felt.

RULES FOR FAVORABLE COMMUNICATION

A. LISTEN

Communicating with your kids is more about listening than it is about speaking, and I mean **really** listening. So often parents listen to what they want to hear and fail to hear what their children really mean. Sound confusing? Here's an example:

Little Billy came into the kitchen as his mother was taking the roast out of the oven. "Mom, where do I come from?" He asked. His mother set the roast on the counter, turned toward him and proceeded to tell the story of the birds and the bees. "No mom, where do I come from?" He asked a second time. Billy's mother sat down on the counter chair next to him. She told the same story, but with more details than she was comfortable with. Billy, still not satisfied, asked again. "Mom, you don't understand. Where do I come from?" His mother, now very uncomfortable with this whole subject, went on to give little Billy explicit details of how babies come about. "Mom, please listen to what I'm saying. Johnny comes from Chicago. Jeffrey comes from Seattle. Where do I come from?"

As you can see by the above story, making assumptions about what a child is saying is fruitless. We don't hear what they are saying, we hear what we are thinking. There's a world of difference between the two. True listening requires the following elements:

GIVE YOUR UNDIVIDED ATTENTION

This means to put down the newspaper, turn off the television, and eliminate any and all other distractions. Look your child in the eyes as he or she speaks. Nod your head once in a while to show that you are interested. Don't look off to the side or make unfavorable

UNDIVIDED ATTENTION

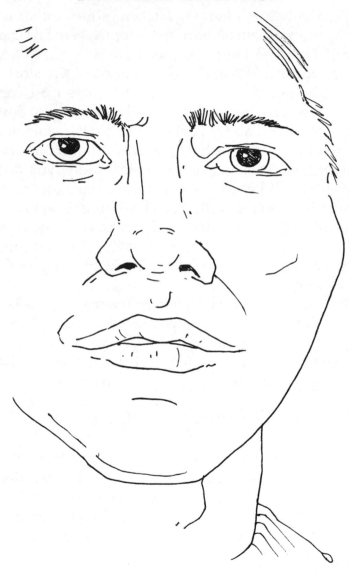

expressions. Stay seated and finish the conversation before you get up to attend to other things.

KEEP AN OPEN MIND

Use empathy when listening. Put yourself in your kid's place and try and follow where he/she is coming from. Don't jump to conclusions before you have heard the child out. What's most important is that you try not to think of what you are going to say before the speaker is finished. Doing this takes your ears off of what is being said and causes you to listen to yourself.

WAIT UNTIL IT'S YOUR TURN

Let your kid finish before you begin to speak. Give some space to what is being said. Interruptions are not only rude, but they cause the person interrupted to feel that what he/she has to say is not being heard.

B. OBSERVE

Keeping your eyes focused on your child as he/she is talking can tell you a lot about what is going on with him or her. Keep in mind that as your kid is talking to you he/she is also observing your reactions.

BE AWARE OF FACIAL EXPRESSIONS AND BODY LANGUAGE

Does your child exhibit signs of uneasiness, such as shifting of body weight, tapping fingers, or stuttering? Parents are intuitive to how their kids are feeling by the way they present their movements. Are they showing signs of being comfortable, such as smiling, good eye contact, and a straight posture? Does anger show? A loud voice, tears, or a scowl on their face? Reading someone's body language and facial expressions can almost tell you more of what that person is saying than words can.

C. RESPOND

How you answer your child will strengthen your relationship as far as communication goes. It sends a direct message to him/her that all went well and that you are open to future discussions.

ANSWER IN A NON-THREATENING WAY

The most efficient way to respond to a child is by vocalizing back in a way that shows you were listening. "I understand what you are saying, and..." or "What you have just said concerns me, because..," are examples of answers that won't put kids on the defensive. Another way is to repeat back to a child what he/she has just told you. And if there is something said that you fail to understand, ask that it be repeated.

I can't count how many times I've heard children tell me that they can't talk to their parents. The reasons they give are many. "They don't listen to me." "My parents don't understand what I want to tell them." "I get yelled at when I try and have a conversation with them." "My parents are too busy to listen to me." Those are only a few that I hear on a weekly basis. When parents ask me what the most important factors are in raising drug-free kids, I tell them, "Listen, listen, and listen." It's that simple.

It's interesting to note that parents tell me almost the same things that the kids do. "My kids never talk to me." "We never have a decent conversation." "They're hardly ever around to discuss anything." "They never hear what I say," and this list goes on. I give the same advice to the kids that I give to the parents. Listen, listen, and listen.

The rules for favorable conversation are for both parties—parents and the kids. It's advisable to sit down with them and go over these rules so that everyone knows what's expected. A breakdown in communication isolates the entire family. When children feel that they are not being heard, they usually feel that they are unwelcome and rejected. What happens next is that most of them will seek acceptance among their peers. Having healthy friendships are good. But when a child feels accepted into an undesirable peer group that may abuse drugs, this is not so good.

Conversations at the dinner table are some of the best moments for a well-bonded family. So is asking children their opinions on family matters. Letting them become involved in the decision-making process in the household lets them know that they are accepted and a responsible part of the family. Research has shown that kids who feel a strong connection to their families are at a low risk of abusing drugs.

THE OPEN-ENDED APPROACH

Using questions as a way to open up conversation with a child is a good way to start building and maintaining a healthy relationship. All of us enjoy talking about ourselves when there is someone present who is interested in what we have to say. The use of closed-ended questions is the worst and most inefficient route to learning about another person. Closed-ended questions lead to a dead end, and quick. Any question that can be answered either "Yes" or "No" is a closed-ended question. It fails to allow the person answering it to go on and explain more. Parents are always at a loss as to why their children only answer "Yeah" or "Nah." It's because they have asked them a question that can only be answered in those terms.

An open-ended question gives the other person per-mission to expand on the conversation. Here is an ex-ample: "Tommy, what was the best thing that happened to you today?" "Oh, I guess it would be when I went over to Robby's house this morning, Dad." "What was it at Robby's house that made it so good, son?" "Well, we watched this neat new video that his mom bought him." "What was the video about?" With open-ended questions, the conversation takes off on it's own power.

Even with an open-ended question, you may hear the standard reply, "I don't know." Carefully decoded, this answer means, "I don't want to talk about it." Some kids don't want to talk about it. Especially if they are used to someone not paying attention or not interested in what they have to say. This can always be followed up with, "I'm interested in hearing what you have to say. Can you tell me why you don't wish to discuss it?" This usually opens the stage up for quality conversa-tion.

GETTING STARTED

If communication is at a standstill in your family, the best way to get it moving again is to get to know each other better. Most parents would balk at this statement. Most would more than likely respond, "I know all about my kid!" But a large proportion of parents would be surprised to find out that what they think they know is far off the mark. This is especially true if there has been little or no communication going on. The following is a list of questions that can get communication opened up again and let each other know something about the other. It takes more than one to play this game, of course. Remember to ask open-ended questions after the initial answers are given. These are only starters to get you off the ground and running. It's best to come up with your own questions once you get back on track to wholesome communication.

- What are the things you are most afraid of?

- Name a moment in your life that was the happiest for you?

- What was the most embarrassing moment in your life?

- If you could improve the world, what would you do?

- What positive qualities do you see in our family?

- What are some of your goals for the future?

- What would be your favorite place to go to?

• Who are some of the people in history that you admire?

• What things would make our family more enjoyable?

• If you had three wishes, what would they be?

So there you have it, resources for opening up dialogue between family members. Practice still makes perfect, so continue to keep the lines of communication open. Involve kids in discussions between you and your friends, and between you and your spouse. Practice it in the car, on the bus, at the baseball game, and everywhere else where it is appropriate to discuss whatever it is you want to discuss. This includes in private, also. The more this happens, the safer and more comfortable everyone feels about discussing those things that cause happiness and those that cause heartbreak. Everyone needs a shoulder to lean on—and an ear to hear them.

Now that you've got the tools for favorable communication, it's time to sit down and discuss drug issues with your kid. Don't fret, it's as simple as it was to learn good rapport between you and your child in the conversation department. A key player in any game never turns and leaves his teammate alone on the field. The key player stands beside his or her kid, regardless of how uncomfortable the game may get. The priority is in winning—not finishing a close second.

TWELVE SUCCESSFUL STEPS TO DISCUSSING DRUGS

Any discussion on drugs should be just that—a discussion. It should be a dialogue between all parties present. As a key player, it will be your responsibility to present the facts on drug use. This includes stating your concerns to your kid, as far as the possibility of his/her becoming involved with drugs at sometime in the future. Don't lecture, whatever you do. Moralizing or preaching about drugs turns kids off. It's the quickest way to put them on the defensive. It has the power to turn their ears off to what it is you're saying. Remember this is a discussion, and you're the key player on your kid's drug-proofing team. This means you're in it together.

Be careful not to use scientific terms or philosophical statements. Talk in layman's terms. Make it as simple to understand as you possibly can. Since kids have short attention spans, keep it short and to the point. You may not have the opportunity to cover all twelve steps in one sitting. If not, continue with the remainder at a later time. It's important to go over these steps periodically as your children grow older. They should be just as important as discussions on sex are.

Find a time and place where there will be the fewest distractions before you begin. Make sure that you have all of your facts straight and up-to-date. The information contained in the chapters before this one are effective resources to use. Give your kid every opportunity to join in with his or her feelings or opinions on drugs and their use, and on any other facts that pertain to drug prevention. This keeps the kid's defenses down and allows him/her to understand that you are on the same team. If you are asked a question that you don't have an answer for, say you don't know. Search for the answer later and convey it to him/her. It is mandatory that this be made to feel like a safe situation. Kids rarely return to places or situations that are uncomfortable or risky. Practicing the "Rules for favorable conversation" will set the scene for a stress-free environment.

The best way to initiate this discussion is to express to your child that you know the world is not a drug-free place. Tell him or her that young people, as well as adults, are exposed to the dangers of drugs almost everyday. Also, that due to different factors and reasons, people make choices that they often regret later. Inform your child that statistics prove that those with the most information and support have the best chances of never becoming involved with drugs. This should open up the door for commencing an effective discussion on drugs. Here are the twelve successful steps to discussing drugs.

1. INQUIRE INTO YOUR KID'S KNOWLEDGE OF DRUGS.

Ask them what they know about drugs and drug use. Parents are usually shocked to hear how knowledge-able their kids are about this subject. They may know how certain drugs affect people, the going prices for street drugs, where they can be obtained. Who sells what, and the slang terms for different drugs. Don't be too dismayed to hear them tell you so much. We live in a very open society and most of what children learn is from television, movies, magazines, music, books, and by watching and listening to others. Unfortunately, a large part of this information is erroneous. Being alert to what they tell you they know can be valuable in help-ing them decipher the accurate from the inaccurate.

Invite them to discuss the drug problem that they may see in their school or elsewhere. How do they feel about it? What do they think should be done about it? Do they have any friends who currently use drugs or have in the past? Do they now or have they in the past known anybody who is or has been in recovery? If they answer "Yes," don't press them to disclose who this person or persons are. This will only tend to make them suspi-cious of your motives and cause them to be tight- lipped from here on out. Be careful not to ask these questions in an interrogating matter. This isn't a court of law. This is a chance to prevent them from using drugs. If they feel uneasy answering some of these questions, go on to the next step. The last thing you want is for this important discussion to end before it even starts.

You may also ask them where they obtained the information that they have. And if they think it is a valid representation of the drug scene. If this step is done with sincerity and concern, it should allay any fears or anxiety that either one of you are feeling.

2. EXPLAIN THE DIFFERENCE BETWEEN GOOD DRUGS AND BAD DRUGS.

Explaining the difference between a drug that is used for the purpose of making a person well again and one that can make one sick is vitally important. Not all drugs are bad or even addictive. The difference between legal and illegal drugs should also be emphasized.

Let your child know that medicines that are sold over the counter or by prescription are essential in helping people get over illnesses. A good example to use is an antibiotic. It's purpose is to eliminate an infection that someone has. Without the use of this drug, the infection could spread, making that person sicker, or possibly causing them to die. Even though antibiotics are legal and prescribed by a doctor, they can still be abused if not taken as directed. Prescription and over-the-counter medicines can harm anyone if too many are taken at once or if they are mixed with other drugs not recommended by a doctor. They should also know that mixing any type of drug with alcohol is dangerous and can be lethal.

Some drugs that are sold legally are not safe. I'm talking about nicotine and alcohol. Explain to your child that both of these substances, although legal, are life-threatening, and harm many people across the country everyday. Point out that even though they are sold on the open market, they are considered illegal when sold to minors. So are prescription drugs when used by someone for whom they weren't prescribed. You can even tell them that some drugs that are considered safe for one person, may not be for another. Over-the-counter and prescription drugs can cause side effects in some people. The good news is that prescription drugs are monitored by the physician who ordered them. This makes them much safer to take than illegal drugs. The effects of drugs, including alcohol, can be unpredictable and hazardous.

3. ILLUSTRATE WHY PEOPLE USE DRUGS.

Children need to be aware of the reasons that people use drugs. Both illegal as well as legal. What you want to convey is that the use of illegal drugs is a conscious choice. That it places sole responsibility in the hands of the one who makes this choice. This includes taking responsibility for any adverse effects that may result.

People take prescription medications for a wide variety of reasons. Diabetics take insulin to control their blood sugar levels. Without this drug, a diabetic could go blind, suffer a stroke, and even die. Someone who is depressed to a point where they don't care whether they live or die is usually given antidepressants to change the chemical structure in their system so that they can maintain a normal attitude. A person with high blood pressure has to take anti-hypertensive medications so their blood pressure will return to normal. This can save them from suffering a fatal heart attack. Legal drugs are meant to get people well and to save lives. Illegal drugs create sickness and often lead to death.

Illegal drugs are used for several different reasons. Some arc them are: Relief of physical and emotional pain, out of boredom, due to peer pressures, curiosity, to feel grown-up, to be happy, to sleep, to stay awake, to speed up, and to slow down. Some take drugs because they have an "I don't care about life" attitude, and others have little or no understanding of the difference between right and wrong. The main point to make is that those that use illegal drugs do so to change the way they feel. They are not satisfied with just being who they really are. They have come to the false conclusion that drugs will make them be somebody else. The problem is that the person taking a drug to accomplish this feat will remain the same person they were—only less healthier than they were before.

Legal drugs such as alcohol, caffeine, and nicotine are used for the same reasons. To change the way one feels. Not everybody who uses alcohol has a problem. Some adults drink in moderation. But alcohol is still considered illegal for a minor to use—even if not abused.

Explain the influences that can cause people to become involved with drugs described earlier in this book. Make it clear that those who are involved in the use of a drug, whether one-time use or more, are not only out to change the way they feel, but are inclined to escape from life. To escape life is to make a poor choice, as it is a temporary illusion that creates a more stressful and troublesome life.

4. INFORM THEM OF THE EFFECTS OF DRUGS.

Kids are more concerned about the short term effects that drugs can have on them. Looking far down the road into the future is a hard concept for them to grasp. Although the emphasis should be on the short term effects, describing the long term effects can give them a general idea of just how devastating drugs can be for a person.

Taking any type of drug has an immediate effect. Once it is ingested, it enters the bloodstream and makes its way to the brain. The effect a drug has on the brain, changes the way a person feels, perceives, and thinks.

The action that a drug may have on one person, may be different in another. This depends on the kind of drug, the amount, and the frequency of use. Other factors are the age, weight, and well-being of the person using the drug. The same drug that may cause one young person to feel high for an extended period of time, may cause another young person to stop breathing, or their heart to cease beating. The effects of any illegal drug can never be predicted with complete certainty.

Using drugs affects not only the physical being of a person, but the emotional nature too. Different drugs can do damage to the kidneys, pancreas, liver, stomach, heart, and brain. They can cause pancreatitis, hepatitis, cirrhosis, ulcers, colitis, seizures, high blood pressure, heart attacks, strokes, and permanent brain damage. Impotence and infertility are a couple more of the effects that drugs can cause, along with a decreased immunity to illnesses and diseases. Birth defects also can be brought on by the use of chemicals. Since almost all young people are self-conscious of their appearance and how others see them, it's important to point out a few more effects. Premature aging, weight gain, weight loss, loss of muscle tone, pale appearance, wrinkles, decayed teeth, brittle hair, skin blemishes, and decreased energy are some of the effects.

The sharing of needles or making illogical decisions regarding sex can bring about the incidence of HIV/ AIDS. Those who use drugs do not usually make rational decisions. Suicides, accidents, and car crashes lead as the prime causes of death in kids. Not to mention accidental overdoses.

Becoming addicted to drugs is also very important to talk about. People who use or experiment with drugs can never tell whether they will become addicted at some time in the future. I don't recall anyone ever telling me that they had a goal in life to be an addict or alcoholic. They all had the same idea that, "It can't happen to me," and before they knew it, it did. Explain that addiction creeps up on people. A person need not be addicted for his or her life to be turned upside down. Addiction compounds the problems that are already brought about by use, misuse, or abuse. It doesn't take years and years to become addicted to a substance. It can happen rapidly, especially in an adolescent. What happens is that the body and the mind crave drugs and a person needs them to reach a normal feeling again. A vicious cycle is then created. The body builds up a tolerance to drugs. This means that it takes more quantities of the same drug to reach an illusive 'normal' plateau. The more drugs one takes, the more severe the addiction. The more severe the addiction, the greater the problems become. It turns into a losing situation. Instead of a person controlling the use of drugs, the drugs control the person. He/she becomes a virtual prisoner to chemicals. Treatment is available to the addict, but not all people are able to stay clean and sober with it. The more advanced the addiction, the more difficult it is to stop.

Other effects to enlighten the child with are the legal ramifications. Again, since drugs lessen a person's logic and reasoning, some decisions are made that are illegal. The majority of those imprisoned today, are there after making wrong decisions under the influence of some chemical. Doing time behind locked doors is not the way to live life. Neither is having to pay off large fines or having a criminal record that can affect future goals and dreams.

The effects of drug use can be felt by others, too. Thousands of innocent people are injured or killed every year by drivers who are under the influence of a mind or mood altering drug. There are different drugs that can cause uncontrollable anger in the user. Our penal institutions are filled by those who have injured or killed someone in a fit of rage, after ingesting drugs. Babies are prone to be born mentally retarded or with learning disabilities due to a mother who uses drugs while pregnant. Relationships with family and friends are difficult to maintain for the drug user. Initiating new relationships is even harder as few people who use drugs have the skills or capabilities needed to begin them.

Be careful when discussing this step that you don't use gory details. Scare tactics have been proven not to work well in prevention efforts. Most people believe that bad things only happen to others, not themselves. This is why it is important to stress, as I have mentioned before, that the initial use of drugs and the effects can happen to anybody. No one is immune from bad things happening in their lives. We have no way of predicting the future.

5. EDUCATE THEM ON WHAT GATEWAY DRUGS
   ARE.

Nicotine, alcohol, and marijuana. These are considered gateway drugs. They are the ones that are almost always used first in a child's lifetime. They are the most widely used and accessible drugs among our young people today. Nicotine is seen as the first and foremost choice of kids out of the three. It stuns me to see the percentage of young people that I work with that smoke cigarettes on a regular basis. I've seen children as young as nine years old that are dependent on cigarettes. Holding a lit cigarette between the fingers or dangling out of the corner of a mouth is considered cool. Children feel that it makes them feel more mature and look grown-up.

Nicotine is a highly addicting drug. It's very difficult to withdraw from it. Most young people have no idea that it is possible to become dependent on it. Some have the idea that if a person smokes only one or two cigarettes a day, there is no harm done. But there is.

Addiction has nothing to do with the amount of drug or drugs used. Some people cross that magical unseen line into addiction after only one or two times of drug use. There's no logical scientific reason for this. It just happens. Who knows why?

Cigarette tobacco contains over 4,000 chemicals. Cigarettes cause over 170,000 deaths a year in the United States. These are mostly attributed to heart disease, emphysema, and cancer. There are also serious risks associated with smoking while pregnant. This can cause low birth weight, pre-term birth, and the possibility of fetal and infant fatalities.

Chewing tobacco is no safer than cigarettes. It has been known to cause jaw and mouth cancer in those who use it. Many kids choose chewing tobacco over smoking, with the belief that it is safer and not addictive. This is untrue. Chewing tobacco contains the same ingredient as cigarettes—nicotine.

Alcohol use by young people usually starts out by sipping a drink or two from a parent or other's drink. It's hard to imagine that a liquid so readily available and legal could be so dangerous. But it is. This drug alone causes more deaths among young persons than any other drug. Alcohol destroys brain cells that can not be replaced. It also puts the liver at risk for developing cirrhosis. Alcohol use by those pregnant can cause mental retardation and other abnormalities in infants. A person does not have to be addicted to alcohol to have problems associated with it's use. Many kids lose their lives every year due to car accidents, drownings, and suicides.

Marijuana is still looked at by this and past generations as a harmless drug. Nothing could be further from the truth. A drug that causes paranoia, psychosis, and memory loss can not be considered safe. There are many more cancer causing agents entering the body by smoking marijuana than from smoking cigarettes. Marijuana has been known to cause sterility in males and can harm an unborn baby if used during pregnancy.

The potency of marijuana has increased over 250% in the last decade. The reasons for this higher potency is due to crossbreeding of plants and added chemicals such as selected drugs and insecticides.

Studies show that people who are not addicted to drugs and don't even use or abuse them, have never used any of the above gateway drugs. Addiction has to start somewhere. Teach your child to resist nicotine, alcohol, and marijuana and the chances of them living a drug-free life are increased greatly.

6. MAKE IT KNOWN THAT THE MAJORITY OF
   KIDS ARE DRUG FREE.

"Everybody's doing it." Ever heard those words before? When it comes to drugs—they're not true. Kids

need to know that not everyone does drugs. In fact, studies have proven that the majority of young people are
drug-free. This is a difficult point to prove to kids. The
reason is that kids who use chemicals usually stand out
like a sore thumb. They take on nicknames like Stoner
or Druggie. Their behaviors are a direct giveaway that
they are users. Most of them are proud of the fact that
they use chemicals, and they make no secret of it. And
there are those who go to great pains to keep their drug
use secret. They often look happy and content on the
outside, but what's going on inside is a different story.
The ones who don't even consider the use of chemicals
are more difficult to spot. They don't demand the attention that most of the users do. At times they seem to
blend into the wallpaper. The fact that they don't have
a large red blinking light on their forehead, reading "I'm
drug-free," makes it hard to know who they are.

Drug-free kids are everywhere. They just need to be
recognized. I always make it mandatory to my patients
in recovery to seek these drug-free kids out and to get
to know them. It follows the old adage, "When you hang
with negative people, you become negative. When you
hang with positive people, you become positive." The
same applies to hanging with clean and sober kids, compared to those that use drugs.

7. MAKE THEM AWARE THAT ABSTINENCE HAS ITS REWARDS.

Being abstinent from mind and mood altering chemicals definitely has its advantages. Quite a few kids feel that they will look stupid or 'nerdy' if they portray a drug-free appearance. Being accepted by their peer group is a big worry for growing kids. If they don't go along with the crowd or look like they're part of the scene, they often feel left out and abandoned. They need to know that living a drug-free life is the key to numerous opportunities at present and in the future.

Being healthy, physically, and emotionally is of vital importance to a maturing child. Emotional security is needed to form satisfying and exciting relationships with others. It gives us empathy, compassion, and the willingness to accept others as they are. It also directs us to value others and to contribute to these relationships on an ongoing basis. The need for good communication and dependability is significant in nurturing and sustaining favorable relationships. Emotional security also plays a powerful part in:

- Learning capabilities

- Fulfilling goals

- Loving oneself and others

- Making rational decisions

Feelings are what guide us along the road of life. When these feelings are changed or eliminated due to the effect of drugs, it impairs decision-making capabilities for immediate and future problems.

Maintaining a sound physical state is what keeps people from having to deal with illnesses or diseases. Kids that consume drugs now may not see the results until months or years later. Since kids are self-conscious of their appearance, let them know that drugs have an upper hand in controlling external impressions. Poor hygiene and a 'could care less attitude' shows in many young people caught up in drug use. Maintaining good health has other advantages, such as:

- Increased energy and strength

- Feeling whole in body, mind, and spirit

- Competition in sports and other activities

- Clearer thinking, retaining, and recalling

- The lack of a healthy body can create a domino effect

• One illness can lead to other illnesses. Many diseases brought on by drug abuse can be chronic,
life-threatening, and eventually fatal.

8. SHOW THEM THAT HAVING FUN IS POSSIBLE
   WITHOUT DRUGS

Ask a young person to give you one good reason that
they use drugs, and the answer will more than likely
be, "To have fun." I believe this to be an honest answer.
Most kids do feel that experimenting or abusing drugs
is fun. At least for a short time, it's fun. But what's the
use of temporary fun, especially when the stakes are
set so high? Having fun isn't about risking your life.
It's not about taking unnecessary chances. It's about
learning how to have fun for the long term. To have fun
is to be happy, joyful, pleased, and gratified.

Children that live recreational lifestyles feel too good
about themselves to get involved with chemicals. Their
self-esteem is high and they have a positive outlook on
things. A person who feels great has little or no thoughts
about changing this. Being joyous and having fun opens
up many doors to life. It takes away stress, anger, and
resentments. Fun is especially important to kids. It
builds character and self-worth.

Fun isn't just about laughing and acting silly. It's about
enjoying oneself. This can be through artistic en-
deavors, helping others, volunteering services,

sports, hobbies, etc. Kids should be taught that using drugs to have fun is like driving a car at a high rate of speed. It's exhilarating, exciting, and it gets the adrenalin pumping— until a brick wall materializes in the middle of the road. Short term fun is just that—short term fun. Drug use is a temporary solution for enjoyable times. The long term solution is found without the use of drugs.

9. RELATE PERSONAL EXPERIENCES.

Sharing your own experiences with drugs can be beneficial in giving kids an honest look at the harm drugs can do. That is, if you once did them. Parents are often afraid to mention any use of drugs by themselves in the past, for fear that it will send the wrong message. This is not true. If your child counters with, "If you did drugs, then what's the big deal with me doing them," let him/her know that it was in the past. Tell your child what you learned from it and how lucky you were to quit. Don't glamorize certain drugs or make light of the subject. Make it plain what did happen and what could have happened beyond that. Explain what it was that made you decide to discontinue using them. Go on to describe how you feel currently about making that decision as well as the accomplishments you've made since then. Kids don't identify well with stories of people, drugs, and problems, unless they can put a face to them or can relate to certain situations.

There are countless stories in magazines, books, newspapers, television, and movies about well known celebrities or sports heroes whose lives have been affected by drugs. Careers have been lost and lives have been lost due to making poor choices concerning drugs.

If you are aware of a friend of yours or a close or distant family member who has had a bad experience with chemicals, get it out into the open. This hits closer to home for kids. It gets their attention and keeps them interested. Real life stories have a dynamic impact on young people.

10. TELL YOUR CHILD THAT HE OR SHE CAN ALWAYS COME TO YOU.

Discussions on drugs should never be a one time deal. It should be ongoing throughout a child's life. Don't let it be a one-sided affair, where you are always the one to bring it up. Tell your child that he or she is welcome to approach you at anytime in the future for another discussion. Say that you would welcome this and that you see this as responsible behavior on their part.

Tell your child that if he/she experiences any type of situation where drugs are involved, to talk about it. If they have any questions, to ask. Most important, if your kid gets in a position where a drug or drugs have been used, let your child know that he/she can come to you. Making yourself available to your kid at all times will make it safer to seek help if he/she gets in a bind.

11. STATE THE FAMILY POLICY ON DRUGS.

Every family needs a policy on drug use. As a parent, you are responsible for setting rules and making sure that they are abided by. Don't use rules and guidelines that are wishy-washy or inconsistent. Make them plain and easy to understand. The best way to do this is to put them down in black and white. This way it can't be disputed that they weren't known or understood. Of course, the entire family will need to be informed of these rules for them to be effective. Go over them, one by one with your child. Make sure he or she is clear on all points. If there is a dispute or disagreement on an issue stated, negotiate it if you feel comfortable. Be sure not to leave any loopholes or contradictions in the wording of this policy.

Explain to your child the reason for a family policy on drugs. Let them know of your concerns for his or her well being and safety in this world. A healthy and strong family has clear and firm boundaries. Fighting over rules is reduced considerably when they are set in stone. This also means that the consequences and punishment for breaking these rules has to be included. Be prepared to carry out these consequences if they are broken. Without enforcement, policies mean little.

The first and most important rule should be very clear: **"Absolutely" no drug use in the home, in a friend's home, or anywhere else.** Point out that this means alcohol, too, and it includes prescription drugs unless prescribed by a doctor. Don't forget about nicotine use, also. It should be made clear that the mere possession of drugs or any related paraphernalia is also a violation of house rules. It's good to make it plain that these rules also apply to anyone visiting in your home.

Leave a situation immediately where there is the presence of drugs. There has been many a kid arrested for being in the wrong place at the wrong time. Any type of association with others who are in possession of illegal drugs puts a person at legal risk. Not to mention the risk of peer pressure on them to participate.

No riding in a vehicle with anyone under the influence of drugs. This should include relatives, baby-sitters, and anyone else. Auto accidents are the chief cause of adolescent fatalities. Many of these deaths involve kids who are innocent victims. Tell them to call you or someone else for a ride if they find themselves in this predicament.

Whereabouts are to be known at all times. Knowing where your children are and what it is they are doing is a parent's responsibility. Kids who keep secrets about their comings and goings are doing something wrong. A person who has nothing to hide—has nothing to hide. It can't be any simpler. Kids who are aware that their parents know their whereabouts are less inclined to be where they're not supposed to be. Keep a list of friend's phone numbers and addresses. Use them.

Friends need to be introduced. Parents need to meet and get to know who their kid's friends are. Since most children have lots of casual acquaintances, it's asking too much to know all of them. The ones that your children spend the most time with, should be introduced to you.

This is also a good time to spell out curfews and other behaviors that are expected by you. Don't make these policies too long or overwhelming. Every parent has their own manner of punishment for unacceptable behaviors. This is something that you will have to give some thought to and make clear to your child.

Writing up a family agreement or contract can be another way of putting these policies in black and white. Here is a sample of one that can give you an idea of what to write.

FAMILY AGREEMENT

I UNDERSTAND FULLY AND AGREE TO THE FOLLOWING RULES SET FORTH IN THIS AGREEMENT:

1. I WILL NOT POSSESS OR USE ALCOHOL OR OTHER DRUGS OR RELATED PARAPHERNALIA IN THIS HOME, A FRIEND'S HOME, OR ANYWHERE ELSE.

2. I WILL IMMEDIATELY LEAVE ANY SITUA-
   TION WHERE THERE ARE DRUGS OR RE-
   LATED PARAPHERNALIA PRESENT.

3. I WILL NOT RIDE AS A PASSENGER IN ANY
   VEHICLE WHEN I HAVE KNOWLEDGE OF
   OR SUSPECT THAT THE DRIVER IS UNDER
   THE INFLUENCE OF ANY MOOD OR MIND
   ALTERING DRUG.

4. I WILL TELL MY PARENTS MY WHERE-
   ABOUTS AT ALL TIMES.

5. I WILL BRING MY CLOSE FRIENDS HOME TO
   BE INTRODUCED.

6. I WILL BE HOME AT 9:00 P.M. WEEKDAYS AND
   12:00 MIDNIGHT ON WEEKENDS.

I UNDERSTAND THAT ANY VIOLATION OF ONE
OR MORE OF THESE RULES WILL RESULT IN ONE
OR MORE OF THE FOLLOWING:

A. LOSS OF DRIVING PRIVILEGES FOR ONE
   WEEK.

B. GROUNDING FOR THREE DAYS.

C. NO USE OF TELEPHONE FOR ONE WEEK.

CHILD'S SIGNATURE

PARENT'S SIGNATURE

PARENT'S SIGNATURE

DATE

I hope that this gives you a general idea of making clear what is expected in your home. As children get older and conditions change, some things can be added or deleted from a written agreement. It's a good idea to go over this periodically and have it posted in a convenient location.

12. TEACH REFUSAL TACTICS.

Teaching kids to say "No" to an offer of drugs sounds like a wonderful concept. Unfortunately, this is far from being effective. Especially when a child feels under pressure from fellow peers. In order to avoid being rejected by other kids, it becomes almost automatic to agree and go along with the crowd. Being accepted by the other kids is part of what growing up is all about. Having to stand alone, outside a circle of peers feels awkward, embarrassing, and uncomfortable for any young person. It becomes easier and less troublesome to say "Yes" instead of "No" for many kids.

Kids that have tactics to deal with dangerous and spontaneous situations do much better at making rational decisions. When a child is put on the spot with no prior rehearsed way out, it's less burdensome to just go along for the ride. Regardless of what the consequences could be. A kid that is ready and waiting for a compromising position, knows how to deal with it at ease. He or she is more able and willing to deal with a surprise situation after each time. This not only keeps kids off of drugs and out of trouble, but builds self-esteem in them at the same time.

The tactics presented below should be practiced between you, your child, and the entire family, as if everyone were competing for an academy award. The more times they are gone over and rehearsed, the more natural it will be for a child to use them when faced with a treacherous situation.

There are six easy to remember tactics that are productive in leaving a situation without having to give in. In my work with groups of chemically dependent kids, these are essential tools to staying clean and sober. The kids split up into smaller groups and each group comes up with an impromptu script. They take turns and use different means and types of pressure to convince each other to do drugs. The kids that are on the refusal side use these tactics presented to gracefully save face and exit the situation. It becomes a lot of fun for everyone that participates. The best part is when some of these same kids come back the next day and say, "Hey, I used those skills that we practiced yesterday, and they worked. I can't believe I turned down an opportunity to get high!"

These six easy tactics used for refusal skills are written to be read by or to your kid. This way they sound more personal and are more empowering to young minds.

A. ASK

The best way to learn is to ask questions. Finding out what lies ahead, gives us ample time to think, plan, and change course if we need to. Very few people that I know of go on a trip without taking a map along. Periodic glancing at this map gives a good indication of where to go and what to avoid. It provides answers that keep us on course, without having to worry about getting lost. When a friend or acquaintance invites you to join in an activity or to go with him or her elsewhere, ask questions.

Friend: "Let's go over to my house. My parents are gone."
You: "What are we going to do there?"
Friend: "Just goof around."
You: "What do you mean by 'goofing around'?"
Friend: "My dad has a bottle of vodka under the sink. We can drink a little of it. He'll never know."

Or:

Friend: "Let's walk back behind the bowling alley,"
You: "What's back there to do?"
Friend: "I've got some killer weed we can smoke."

Asking questions gives you a clear vision of what is involved if you comply. If it involves a situation that is unsafe or one that you feel uncomfortable with, the next tactic is then used.

B. THINK

Using logic and reasoning has saved more lives than anything else. The best way to use these two principles is to question yourself.

"What could the consequences be?"

"Is this wrong?"

"Could I get in trouble?"

"Can this hurt me?"

"Does this go against my morals and values?"

"What have I been taught or learned about this be
    fore?"

"Will I regret this later?"

Impulsive decisions are usually regretted later. Take
your time and assess the situation at hand. Three important things to do are: Think—Think—Think. If you
feel that what is asked of you is wrong and you would
just as soon not do it, then go on to the next tactic.

C. IF IT IS WRONG—SAY SO

Assertive behavior is the way to protect yourself. It
shows personal responsibility.

"No, that's OK. I don't smoke pot."

"I could get grounded for that if my folks found out."

"I don't use the stuff, myself."

"That's not cool for me."

"No way! That's gross!"

Stand up for yourself. Peer pressure is nothing but an invisible bully. It has no power over you. Say it the way it is—whatever is on your mind. This is where those feelings of possible rejection or embarrassment seep in. There's nothing worse than being alone. The best way to handle this is to turn the tables and take control of the situation. No one will ever be wise to what you are doing. To accomplish this, follow the next tactic.

D. SUGGEST SOMETHING ELSE TO DO

Knowing that you have choices and alternatives for different situations puts you in the driver's seat. They open up new opportunities for growth. It's kind of like having a square peg with one round hole and several square ones. You can try as you might to push, pound, and squeeze the peg into the one wrong hole, or you can gently set it into the nearest correct one.

By suggesting something else to do, you take your-self out of the front lines. You also give the other person a chance to see that there are other opportunities, too.

"Let's go down to the high school gym and shoot hoops."

"There's an awesome new movie playing downtown. Want to go?"

"We can go over to my house for awhile."

"How about us going over to a friend of mine's house?"

If all goes well, you've diverted the other person's attention away from the unwholesome offer that they originally brought up. Everybody likes good clean fun. How could anyone turn down offers like these? I'm not sure how, but it does happen. You may hear, "No, thanks. Let's just go get stoned." Worse yet, it could be, "Be a wimp if you want. I'm going to get high." Don't let this deter your plans of continuing to refuse what it is you don't wish to do. Keep thinking and remember that you are still in control. Follow the next tactic.

E.   OFFER A SECOND CHANCE

Most people believe in giving second chances. I know I do. And when it comes to saying "No," it will set your mind at ease that you did all that you could do if the offer is again refused.

What you want to do is to let the other person know that you are leaving the door open. That your invitation still stands even if you walk away. The other person may need time to think. He or she may not want to risk looking soft instead of tough. This next tactic is the last and final offer.

"If you change your mind, I'll be at the high school gym."

"Call me later if you want to go do something else."

"I'll see you later, if you don't have anything to do."

"Meet me at the movies. That's where I'll be."

"I'm going over to the mall. Feel free to join me."

This may work and it may not. If it does, great!

Now it's your turn to introduce the other person to a satisfying life without the need for drugs. But what if the answer is still, "No way!?" Then it's time to do the next best thing. Read on.

F. LEAVE

What could be more simple? You turn the other direction and walk away. Presto! You're out of the situation. You gave it your best shot. You checked out the scene, thought about it, took personal responsibility, asserted yourself, offered something different, and then terminated the conversation. You walked away. Now it's time to look at what it was you did and take pride in this feat. You may have just made a lifesaving decision. You probably got yourself out of trouble before you got into it. This more than likely saved you a whole lot of stress later, and you lived to remember it.

Use these skills as a guideline to come up with different situations, questions, and answers. Take turns in being the good guy and the bad guy. Turn it into a game if you want. The more fun that your kid gets out of it, the more ingrained it will become in his or her memory. Challenge your child to use these skills every time the opportunity presents itself. This isn't to say that he/she should go looking for an occasion to try them out. But surprises do happen. Kids can never be sure when someone may offer them a line of cocaine or a hit of crank.

A DRUG FREE AMERICA

Preventive measures such as the ones just presented are the answers to keeping kids drug-free. It may take an entire generation or two to wipe out adolescent drug use in America, but it has to start somewhere. That somewhere begins with you playing a key part on your own kid's drug-proofing team. It was once said that, "A tall building begins with a handful of dirt. A large redwood tree begins from a tiny seed. A walk of a thousand miles begins with one footstep." I believe that a drug-free life for young people begins with a key player. Someone with leadership qualities that can direct the right moves and plays for a winning game. Being that key player yourself, and playing on your kid's drug-proofing team, you do have the power to start the ball rolling toward a drug-free America.

VI

PREVENTING THE WORST OF THE WORST—SUICIDE

No book on drug prevention for young people would be complete without a chapter on suicide. This word makes many parents uncomfortable and can send chills up and down the spine of anyone. The reason I have included it is simple—suicide among kids is rising at an alarming rate. It is said that well over 70% of teenage suicides involve the use of drugs. Whether drugs are involved or not, it's always a good idea to learn what you can about this horrible subject and the ways to prevent it from happening. Thoughts of suicide brought on by pressures and stress can make a big difference in a child's decision to use or abuse drugs or abstain from them.

How prevalent is suicide among the young? Consider this—Every 90 minutes in this country, a teen commits suicide. Every 60 seconds, a teen attempts to take their own life. Suicide rates among kids have quadrupled since 1950. As you can see, this is an important subject to know and to understand. Let's look at some other facts associated with suicide and kids:

• Suicides are more dominant in the western states.

• Springtime is when suicide rates climb.

• The risk of suicide is increased when there is unresolved conflict within the family.

• Illness or disability increases the risk of suicide.

• The risk of suicide increases greatly when alcohol or other drugs are involved.

• Homosexuals and bisexuals are seven times more likely to commit suicide.

• Childhood abuse is a large factor in suicides.

• One in five teens will consider or attempt suicide.

• A published poll among Medical Examiners showed that over 50% of them believed that suicide rates among the young could be understated. That the actual rates could be twice as high.

• Suicide among young people is more common among males than females.

Studies show that in a high school class of 30 students, two or three of them have attempted to take their own lives.

Native Americans between the ages of 15 and 20 are 10 times more likely to commit suicide than any other culture.

Those from a family with a history of mental illness may be more prone to suicide.

It is not uncommon for small children to take their own lives.

SUICIDE—WHAT IS IT AND WHAT CAUSES IT?

Suicide is what I describe as "Life versus life." It's a personal choice followed by a deliberate act of ending one's own life. The final escape. The final drop out from life.

WHAT IT'S NOT

A disease

A virus

An accident

Inherited

An emotional disorder

A compulsion

WHAT OTHERS HAVE TO SAY ABOUT IT

"Suicide often arises not from a hatred of life, but from a lust for it, a desire for things to be otherwise, for life to be full when it appears not to be." Stephen Levine

"About 90% of suicidal teenagers feel their families don't understand them. And when they express their feelings of unhappiness, frustration, or failure, the teenagers say their families either ignore, deny, or attack those feelings." The Youth Ministry Resource Book

"A suicide is a person who has considered his own case and decided that he is worthless and who acts as his own judge, jury, and executioner and he probably knows better than anyone else whether there is justice in the verdict." Don Marquis

"Suicide stems from feelings of aggression turned inward, toward the self." Sigmund Freud

"The ultimate protest." John Langone

"Without doubt worse still is he who kills himself, because there is none nearer to a man than himself."

St. Augustine

"The tragedy of life, my friend, is not that it must end. But that so many times before our natural demise, we must wish for death."

Anonymous Greek philosopher

GETTING THE STORY STRAIGHT

It troubles me to see so much wrong information out there concerning this subject that takes so many lives. People tend to believe what they hear without checking out whether it is true or not. Some of these untruths were listed above. Now I'll go over some other erroneous information that I still hear parents talking about, and try to set the record straight.

KIDS WHO TALK ABOUT IT NEVER REALLY FOLLOW THROUGH

Don't believe this for a second. A young person who talks about taking their own life is at a high risk for following through with it. This should be taken seriously and help rendered to the individual. Any reference to or threat of suicide is a desperate and possibly last ditch effort at asking for help.

When I inform a parent that their child has made an indication of intentionally harming him or herself, it's often met with, "That's just an attention getter." They're right. This is an attention getter. It's a possible plea for aid. One can never be too sure. I would hate to be the one to brush it off and then learn later that a life was taken. We all remember the story of "The boy who cried wolf." That was a fairy tale. This is Real Life 101.

ONLY EMOTIONALLY UNBALANCED KIDS COMMIT SUICIDE

Kids who are emotionally well-balanced and highly intelligent can and do end their own lives. They may get to the point where they are unable to cope with the pressures that often make their way into their lives. The lack of adequate coping skills and the inability to reduce stress can give some the belief that things will never get better.

The use of drugs can create confusing thoughts and wrong ideas. This often leads a person to make irrational decisions about their life. It's difficult to look at other alternatives and choices when your thoughts are being ruled by mood and mind altering chemicals.

SUICIDE IS IMPULSIVE AND HAPPENS WITHOUT FOREWARNING

A kid doesn't just happen to wake up one morning and decide to commit suicide. There are numerous factors that lead up to it. It's not an idea or thought that appears out of the clear blue sky.

There are signs and symptoms that young people usually exhibit before they make an attempt on their lives. These are red flags that alert parents and others to take action to see that a possible suicide is averted. The knowledge of drug use by a child is cause to be concerned.

AFTER A KID ATTEMPTS SUICIDE, THE RISK DECREASES

Once any attempt at suicide is made, the risk of completing the act becomes greater. Over 40% of young people who lose their lives due to suicide, have attempted it before. Some people will make attempt after attempt before carrying through with taking their own lives. This could be a way of calling out for help.

SUICIDE IS CLASSIFIED AS A FATAL ILLNESS

There is absolutely no evidence that suicide is an emotional or physical illness or disease. It can however, be brought on by other illnesses or diseases. Pain, fear, or an unpredictable outlook brought on by any type of sickness could lead one to take his/her own life instead of accepting and dealing with the problem at hand. Suicide can best be described as a behavior that is life threatening.

SUICIDAL KIDS SHOULD BE TOLD TO "CHEER UP"

This can actually do more harm than good. Suicidal thoughts are not that simple to relieve. A person thinking about suicide is at that point because he or she has a problem attaining cheerfulness. Being at a point of hopelessness gives the suicidal person a hazy outlook at the possibility of changing the way he/she feels. Saying to them, "Cheer up," is futile.

A person with thoughts of suicide feel that he/she has enough problems as it is. When told to "Cheer up," feelings of guilt and shame could be overwhelming. This could tend to create more hostility within the child and could possibly drive him/her closer to self destruction.

THOSE WHO ARE SUICIDAL WILL ALWAYS BE SUICIDAL

There is hope for everybody. This is regardless of the problems a person may have. With proper and efficient therapy, kids with thoughts of suicide or previous attempts can and often do get better. Once they find a purpose and worth within themselves, the last thing they wish for is to die. Medications are also available for those who are plagued by depression or other emotional illnesses. For kids who are abusing or are addicted to drugs, it's a simple matter of getting them clean and sober.

THE DARK SHADOW OF DEPRESSION

Depression is nothing new. It's been around since the beginning of time, and affects millions of people every day. "Feeling down in the dumps," or "Having the blues," for an extended period of time is the prime factor in suicides among the young. The presence of this dark shadow can be eliminated with proper counseling or therapy for most kids. Over 90% do recover from it. The word depression comes from the old romantic sounding term, melancholy. Melancholy in Greek means "Black bile." That's what depression is all about. It's as though a deep darkness has descended on the one affected by it.

Depression in children can be caused by many different things. Some of these could be:

• The loss of someone or something significant

• Mood disorders such as bipolar disorder

• Drugs—illegal and legal

• Damage or trauma to the brain

• Infectious diseases

• Sexual identity problems—homosexuality

• School failures

• Rejection by peers

• World worries—AIDS, global warming, nuclear weapons, etc.

• Health worries of self or others

When a person becomes depressed and continues in this state of mind for a prolonged period of time, it sets the stage for three progressive elements. These elements often lead to initial thoughts of suicide and could advance to the taking of one's own life. In order of progression, they are:

HAPLESSNESS

This is where the person feels that everything seems to go wrong in his/her life. Many have the idea that "bad luck" runs in their blood. That regardless of what they do, nothing will ever change. The idea or perception that life has dealt them a bad hand of cards pervades their thoughts.

HELPLESSNESS

An attitude that there is no way out of the problems that affect a person. The young person may look around for options but not be able to see any. The child feels that he/she is the only one that can solve the problem, and fail to realize that reaching out to others can help.

HOPELESSNESS

This is known as the "Giving up" stage. It is the final belief and acceptance that there is absolutely no way out. That everything that can go wrong will and that nothing can be done to change it.

After the "giving up" stage comes a deeper darkness than ever before. A child comes to what they feel is the end of the road, where there is no purpose or use in going on living.

THE CRIES FOR HELP

Suicidal kids tend to make an attempt at letting others know that they are in an emotional bind. The warning signs that are exhibited can sometimes be recognized if it is known what to listen and look for. All of the listed "Cries for help" should be taken seriously and immediate assistance found for the person who exhibits them.

• Depression—Any signs of haplessness, helplessness, or hopelessness

• Verbal statements of intentions—Such as "I wish I were dead." "I can't take life anymore." "I might as well kill myself."

• Psychosomatic health complaints

• Withdrawal from family and friends

• Any noticed personal loss, separation, or grief

• Verbal related fears of health problems, medical tests, scheduled hospitalization

• Giving up of personal possessions

• Drastic change in eating and sleeping habits

• Marked change in mood or attitude

• Verbal statements of loneliness or of not being loved

• Marked neglect of personal appearance

• Loss of concentration

• Verbal statements of worthlessness

• Preoccupation with thoughts of death

Seeing any of these symptoms is indication enough to warrant an intervention in any young person's life. Kids who cry out for help feel at a loss in knowing how to change the way they feel. A cry for help is a way of saying "I hope you notice me and do something".

RESPONDING TO THE CRIES

Taking action to help anyone that exhibits these cries should be immediate. Putting off a response due to the attitude that it may go away tomorrow, could result in the action being too late.

WHAT TO DO

• Take it seriously—When a child informs you that they are considering taking their own life—believe them!

• Listen to them—Give your utmost attention without overreacting or interrupting.

• Accept them—Kids who are suicidal feel 'apart from.' They feel that there is no one that understands them. Validate these feelings.

• Get details—Ask what specific things are bothering them. Use open-ended questions that can't be answered simply 'yes' or 'no.'

• Suggest options- Ask, "What other options or choices are there to deal with this problem?" Remind them that problems are temporary and can be overcome.

• Use silence—When there is silence and you don't know what to say next—say nothing. Silence allows both parties to think.

• Allow ownership—Let the other person come up with their own answers for their problems. This builds self-worth.

• Assess worth—Ask what still matters in their life. What has value and meaning to them?

• Determine intent—Ask if the person has a plan and the means to carry it out.

• Agreement—Have the person agree to not harm themself until they follow through with extended help.

• Show care—Ask, "What would you like for me to do to help you?"

• **SEEK HELP**—Immediately call a local Crisis Response Center, Mental Health Clinic, Hospital, or Doctor.

There are also those things that can do more harm than good for a suicidal child. The following list are those specifics that should be avoided when dealing with this life and death situation.

WHAT NOT TO DO

- Criticize—Telling someone that they are 'stupid' or 'crazy' is dangerous. A suicidal child feels that he or she has no control over feelings of hopelessness.

- Promise—Promising that things will be much brighter and better tomorrow sounds good—but it may not come true.

- Threaten—This only tends to bring the suicidal child closer to the task intended. It could even make him or her think, "Oh yeah? Let's see about that!"

- Shame—Telling the young person that their sui cide will only cause pain and hurt for others could push the child over the edge. This is especially true if his or her suicide is planned to hurt others.

- Invalidate—Don't try to convince the person that his or her problems are insignificant compared to other's problems.

• LEAVE ALONE—Never leave the person alone while in a suicidal frame of mind. Stay by their side until outside help can be established. This is essential if a specific plan has been mentioned.

INDICATIONS OF DEPRESSION

The recognition of depression in kids can tip you off that something is wrong before they progress to a suicidal state. Not everyone who is depressed becomes suicidal. But even in non-suicidal kids, depression can create a downward spiral as far as their emotional and physical heath is concerned. Depression can affect anyone, regardless of age. Even small infants experience periods of gloom. Identifying and talking about symptoms of depression can head off a potential disaster somewhere down the road. These are the signs to be alert to:

TODDLERS AND PRE-SCHOOLERS

• Regression—Regressing to earlier patterns, such as thumb sucking, bedwetting, etc.

• Sleep problems—Problems with falling asleep. Nightmares. A constant desire to sleep in a parent's bed.

• Attention seeking—Acting out in violent or angry ways, such as biting, kicking, hitting, breaking objects, and screaming.

YOUNG CHILDREN—UP TO 12

• Sadness—An obviously sad or forsaken look.

• Lack of motivation—The lack of energy or desire to complete assignments or responsibilities.

• Withdrawal—A change from being involved in activities to withdrawal from them. Spending excessive time alone.

TEENS—UP TO 19

• Lack of hope for future—An attitude or outlook that the future does not matter. No plans or goals past each current day.

• Drug abuse—Drugs are often used to deal with any feelings of depression.

• Change in eating habits—A drastic change, either overeating or eating too little. Depression can be a major cause of eating disorders.

Any young person who shows signs of depression should be given a physical examination by a physician and followed up by a psychological evaluation if recommended. This is especially true if the symptoms are not short term. Life has a tendency to give us all the 'blues' every once in a while. Some of us, including kids, bounce back out of this in no time. Others get caught up in it and don't recover on their own. This is when some type of professional help is needed.

ENCOURAGING LIFE IN YOUR KIDS

What's the best way of reducing the risk of adolescent depression and suicide? It's by encouraging life in the adolescent so that they don't have to feel that it's discouraging. If your kid is depressed due to drug use, a program of recovery may be all that is needed. For others, it may mean working with them at problem solving skills or stress reduction. And for some, a warm and caring shoulder to cry on may do the trick. The "Life plan" presented below can give your children a vision of hope and value in their precious lives if they seem to be experiencing a life void of gratitude.

A.   TEACH THAT LIFE HAS MEANING

We are all unique individuals with special talents. Some of us have no idea what those talents may be at the present. Some day we will. There is a universal plan for each one of us. That plan is in motion right now in our lives, and we may not even know what it is. The phrase, "More will be revealed," should give us comfort that with patience, we come to find out.

B. SHOW THE MORAL OBJECTIONS TO SUICIDE

The taking of one's own life is wrong. It goes against nature and the purpose for our existence. We were given this life for a reason and it is not for us to determine whether it should be eliminated.

C. EXPLAIN OUR RESPONSIBILITY TO OTHERS

We're not on this earth just for ourselves. Life would be dull and boring if this were true. Each one of us has a responsibility to our family, friends, and to others. They need us as much as we need them. It is our responsibility to teach others, just as it is our responsibility to learn from others.

D. ILLUSTRATE THAT STRENGTH COMES FROM WEAKNESS

The opposite of dark is light. We are not immune to emotional and physical hurt and pain. They are a part of life. These are only temporary feelings that do go away. Each time that we are able to get through them, we become stronger in our faith in the future.

Suicide is a permanent solution to a temporary problem. Kids need to see that temporary problems mean just that —temporary. They can be resolved or accepted. Drugs are not the answer in dealing with depression. They may hide what it is that is bothering a young person, but only for a short time. In the long run, the initial problem gives birth to many other ones.

A key player can be instrumental in showing a young person that solutions to life's problems and worries can be found. They need to know that 'feelings of darkness' do go away. That there are other methods of coping with them, besides the use of drugs or other self-destructive methods.

BUILD A LOVING RELATIONSHIP

VII

BEING A KEY PLAYER ON YOUR KID'S DRUG-PROOFING TEAM

One of the most challenging tasks of any parent today, is raising children to be drug-free. It seems at times that there are too many evils working against us in our fight to keep them healthy. This book has been designed for that explicit purpose. I've shown how the greatest enemy of our lifetime can be fought and overcome. We must never close our eyes to this continuing war on drugs. They have ruined too many young lives, families, friends, and communities. It is our responsibility to persist in this fight, and to move forward. To not give up until all kids have come to the realization that it's OK to be who they are without the need to be someone else. That to change who they are is a temporary solution that has the potential of becoming a long term problem.

Being a key player on your kid's drug-proofing team means never giving up the fight. At least not as long as your kid's life is being challenged by the threat of drugs. It means putting a winning effort into building a loving relationship with your child. Teaching him/her to feel good about themself. Laying down a path to follow into a secure future.

This chapter is about staying active as a key player on your kid's drug-proofing team. It's about what you as a parent can do to foster self-worth in your child. I never see kids in my practice who walk in the door for the first time feeling on top of the world. Rarely do I see smiles or hear laughter. What I see are kids that have been beaten down by the power of drugs. Kids who feel sadness, confusion, and are spiritually bankrupt. The better a child feels about him or herself, the more responsibility taken for his or her life. This leads to personal strengths that are needed to overcome the trials and tribulations that are a part of life. A key player needs to know and understand how to play the game from the heart. This needs to be ongoing. To think that you've won the game before it's over is dangerous thinking. Don't retire to the bench just yet. Resume your task as a key player. Your kid can always use you on the team.

Drug prevention efforts need to expand beyond the playing field. Community support is equally important in the raising of drug-free children. We may be able to keep this monster (drugs) at bay and away from our children, but it takes a crowd to drive it away for good. We'll look at those things that can be done to make your community safer for the kids. But first, let's see what's needed for staying active in raising drug-free kids.

RAISING KIDS FROM THE HEART

Telling your kids often that you love them is a major component in healthy parent-child relationships. These three words, 'I love you,' spoken from the heart, can generate healing from a scraped knee to the loss felt for a best friend who moves away. Is the recital of these beautiful words enough? Is there more to it? Abigail Adams once said, "We have too many high sounding words, and too few actions that correspond with them."

Young people have incredible awareness abilities and often take notice of our actions toward them as well as of the words we speak. Actions serve to demonstrate the proof in what is said. They speak much louder than words.

A key player needs to parent from the heart. This means to give your kid the most loving attention that you can. It also means being aware of certain personal traits that have a direct effect on them. Parents are never perfect. We're far from that. We sometimes show undesirable behaviors that are picked up by our kids like a spy plane taking aerial photographs of enemy territory. Thinking that they don't notice, we go about our business while they click away with the camera. Your kid may forget to take out the garbage on a weekly basis, but believe me, he or she won't forget any objectionable moves you make.

They see and they remember. This is stored in their memory banks and is either brought up later as a weapon of revenge ("But that's not what you do, dad.") or it passively gives them permission to do the same.

The old, "Don't do what I do—do as I say," just doesn't cut it. Any parent that thinks that his or her kid will behave in a different way than he does is mistaken. Children learn from our words and our actions. I'll explain what I feel are important actions that a key player should take.

BE A POSITIVE MODEL

Children often imitate their parents. The younger they are, the more this is true. Little kids spend quality time dressing up like mom and dad. We all remember playing house when we were young, don't we? It was learned from watching and being aware of our own parents, and it was taken seriously.

You are the most important teacher that your child will ever know. This not only means in the skills that are taught by you, but in the way you model your own life. You can't seriously expect your child to be honest if each time the phone rang, you yelled, "If it's for me, tell them I'm not here." This may sound like a little white lie and sort of trivial, but it isn't. Little lies turn into big lies. Honesty means being truthful 100% of the time. Could you imagine teaching your child that honesty is the best policy, but there will be times when a lie is justified? That sometimes there will be circumstances that will warrant dishonesty? I hope not. Honesty needs to be practiced in all of our affairs if we expect our kids to follow this same virtue.

If you expect your kid not to experiment with mood or mind altering drugs, set an example by refraining from them yourself. Explain the reasons that you choose not to do them. Parents frequently ask me if it is a poor choice for them to have a beer or a drink once in a great while in front of the kids. My opinion is that it is. Seeing the destruction that chemicals have had on the young people in this world is reason enough for me to do without alcohol. This is one substance that I can definitely do without—all in the name of sober healthy kids.

What virtues have been most important in your life? Do you believe and practice equality among all people? Regardless of color, creed, religion, or sex? Is faith meaningful to you? These are things that need to be looked at. Children learn morals and values from moms and dads. Years ago, they were taught step by step to each child in the home. Today, that rarely happens. Most parents are too busy scurrying to and fro to sit down and spend hours with their children. Some parents have no idea what proper morals and values are, because they were never taught to them. Parents who model morality on a daily basis are teaching their children the same. Some things that I have always tried to keep in mind are:

- Am I living the same life that I wish for my children to live?

- Am I walking the walk of what I talk?

- Do I admit to my kids when I am wrong?

- Are my actions consistent with what I expect of them?

- What must I change for them to change?

Taking a personal inventory of your behaviors and actions can do wonders in bringing up drug-free kids. I've even seen parents model after their own children. Some patients that I have worked with that have made dramatic turnarounds in their sobriety, have talked about how their parents changed after they did. We all have something to learn from one another. But it's our responsibility as parents to teach them first. Not to expect them to learn elsewhere and to then teach us.

ACCEPT YOUR KIDS AS THEY ARE

I've said it before and I'll say it again—we are not perfect. Neither are our children. And we shouldn't expect them to be. All children are unique and special and gifted in their own ways. Scores of parents fail to see the good in their kids. They quite often focus on the character flaws and completely overlook the beauty that is tucked safely inside.

You may not always like or agree with some of the things that your kids do, whether it's a rock band that they worship or the use of drugs. Accept them anyway. Holding on to old resentments or anger fostered by a child's past or present behavior gets nobody anywhere. Granted, it's not easy practicing acceptance for a kid who goes totally against a parent's wishes. But when the love for that child stops, so does healthy growth. Growth for both of you.

Probably the two most misunderstood words in the English language are "Unconditional love." To have unconditional love for another person is more difficult to do than just have 'love' for that person. It goes beyond this. It means to love your kid no matter what he/she has done. Regardless of any unspeakable acts that may have been committed. No excuses. No exceptions. It means requiring nothing in return. No expectations. One hundred percent unconditional love—period!

You may be thinking, "But won't this send the wrong message to my kid? Isn't this the same as condoning what it may be that was done wrong?" No! You're not saying that you agree. That you don't care. That you wish the kid luck on continuing to do what it is he/she is doing. It's simply letting the child know that you love him or her, even under extreme conditions. This doesn't mean to not hold the youngster accountable for his/her actions or to give up on punishing for wrong-doing. It simply means that you love your son or daughter. The message it conveys is that even though he/she may have screwed up (maybe big time) you still love your child and trust that better choices will be made next time. Kids slip up at times. I wouldn't even care to count how many times that I've screwed up. How about you? The next step is to show your kid how to avoid making the same mistake again. If we never made mistakes, we would have no lessons to learn. And lessons are the things that teach us how to grow in leaps and bounds.

ENCOURAGE YOUR CHILDREN

Encouragement on an ongoing basis builds self-esteem and self-worth in a child. It is impossible for a kid to feel that he or she is appreciated, responsible, and valuable without encouragement. Adding this is like adding fuel to their drive to persistently go beyond what has worked for the child before. It's almost like winning a foot race. If you know that you won the race because you ran the fastest, you're likely going to run even faster next time. You know that this will give you an even better edge over the previous run. It's insurance that the risk of losing will be kept to a minimum.

Giving praise can be wonderful, but encouragement is much more powerful and effective. To encourage children is to promote the precious personal gifts that they each possess. Don't look only for major accomplishments, but for the small achievements, too. Let children know that you appreciate each good deed that is done. Tell them why you are appreciative and encourage them to continue on. Do this in different areas of their lives. Try not to center your attention on one or two good points. Look real hard and I guarantee you will see much more than you ever expected. Many a parent has shed tears after going through a family chemical dependency session and has seen the value in their child that they lost sight of long ago. What they see is but the tip of the iceberg. Daily encouragement can and does reveal much more.

Can you imagine working a forty hour a week job without anyone noticing or encouraging you? Would you feel prideful and willing to put more into your work than was expected of you? Would you be happy and satisfied in this situation? I can't imagine anyone not feeling invalidated and unworthy. A kid's life is the same way. No encouragement—no growth.

SHOW THEM RESPECT

The only way that children can grow emotionally is if they have the space to form their own opinions. You may not agree with every one of them. In fact you may be downright offended by some of them. Respect your children anyway. If you see that they have a viewpoint that is dangerous or goes against good values and morals, inform them how you feel about it. Don't criticize or condemn them for their thoughts. They may not know both sides of the coin. Express what you know about the subject and add to their knowledge. Show the pros and the cons.

"He doesn't respect me, so why should I respect him?" I've probably heard those words a thousand times. Both from parents and kids. Someone has to be humble enough to put their foot forward and start showing respect before the other person is usually willing to do the same. This sounds like a silly childish game, but it happens in the best of families. It's standoffs like these that can make relationships crumble.

Showing respect shows that you're proud of your kid. It sends a silent message to him or her that what he/she is doing is met by approval. It shows that you're satisfied with the decisions that they have made. Showing respect is much like showing enthusiasm. It builds strong bonds between children and parents.

LOVE THEM FROM THE HEART

It's easy to say "I love you." And it's vitally important to say these comforting words to your kids. What's more important is to show them through the loving deeds described above. The actions that you put forward today toward your kids, from your heart, will be mirrored by them for the rest of their lives. Kids that are accepted, encouraged, respected, and told that they are loved are seldom those who experiment with dangerous and illegal substances. Especially if they have positive role models to follow—their parents.

COMMUNITY ACTION

As I said earlier, being involved in efforts to make your community safer for adolescents is just as important as raising them from the heart. Unless your child is a virtual prisoner in his or her own home, he/she will be exposed to drugs somewhere, sometime, in the community. There's no possible way of getting around this unless all drugs were to disappear off the face of the earth. That's highly unlikely to happen by tomorrow. There are ways that you can become active in your community to lower the risk of drugs becoming a problem for your child. First, it's important to find out where your community stands as far as adolescent drug prevention goes. Then it's time to make changes, if they're warranted. A team player always looks at what's best for the rest of the team. To make it more simple, I'll break it down into different areas.

SCHOOLS

Does each school have a detailed and specific policy on the use of drugs? Most schools that recognize the national problem with kids and drugs do. They normally have what is called a "Zero tolerance policy." This means that any and all drugs and the use of them is absolutely forbidden. There are no exceptions. The policies always state in black and white what the consequences are for violating this rule. As with any policy, it needs to be enforced to work. Ask the school if it is. Are children that are found in violation of it required to be evaluated for a possible drug problem? And most important, is it followed through so that any recommendations that may be made are implemented? Most schools fall short on this point. I've seen them do an excellent job of dishing out the punishments, and requiring a drug evaluation. Unfortunately, it sometimes stops there. Recommendations for treatment to help kids are often ignored and not enforced. These kids that fall through the cracks are the ones who re-offend. They're not going to change unless their personal situation changes.

Is a drug curriculum taught to students in class? Has it been effective? As with old outdated schoolbooks, some of the information that is being taught is old hat. A lot of it doesn't apply today. The field of chemical dependency is changing all of the time. Resources need to be updated on a continuing basis.

Are staff members aware of what to look for? Do they know how to handle a drug using situation? Are parents being informed of a suspected or definite drug problem seen in their children? Schools need to hold regular workshops and training sessions for staff members to be effective in recognizing and getting help for kids with drug problems. Counselors should be available to those students who need to talk or need help concerning drugs.

Does the school sponsor drug-free activities? Dances, sports, and other activities that are heavily chaperoned with strict rules against drug use are strongly encouraged. They give students the message that fun can be had without the use of chemicals.

BUSINESSES

Local businesses can be empowering in the prevention of drug use by kids. They are able to financially support efforts needed in dollars, supplies, and services.

Do they see the drug problem that exists? Are they willing to sponsor drug-free activities for kids? Will they publicly take a stand for a vision of a drug-free community?

Do they inform employees of the dangers of drugs and kids? Are counseling resources made available for families in need? Does it have an Employee Assistance Program? Education and support for adults can be a mighty tool in drug prevention efforts. Is information being handed out to employees about the dangers of drugs within the community? Some parents are not aware of the scope of the problem.

Are there businesses that are known for selling alcohol or nicotine to minors? Have they been made aware that this needs to stop or they will have legal problems? Businesses need patrons to keep operating. A parent or group of parents has an obligation to put pressure on any business that contributes to the drug problem.

MEDIA AND PRESS

This is a vehicle that has great potential for promoting a drug-free message. Is it doing this? Are public service announcements on prevention being aired? Are stories of drug use being glorified or sensationalized? Media representatives rarely ignore the concerns of the public. There are stories of how only a few persons have made an impact by complaining about inappropriate coverage and messages. If you feel that what you see and hear on television, radio, or the printed page, is giving the wrong message, let your voice be heard. Suggest options such as showing the dangers of drug use and how to protect young people from these dangers.

Are local talk shows or reporters interviewing professionals in the chemical dependency field? Are they covering and promoting drug-free activities? Discuss your concerns and offer suggestions to program managers and editorial staff.

The editorial section of any newspaper is there for anyone to voice their opinion. Letters sent to the editor stating your views on the drug problem and ways to combat it are essential. Letter writing campaigns by a group of parents involved in prevention efforts is even more influential.

POLITICAL

Are city, county, and state officials aware of the drug problem? What are they doing to promote prevention efforts? Elected officials are there to serve you, the voter. Arrange for someone to speak at one of their regular scheduled meetings or workshops.

Do some laws need to be changed or implemented to insure a safer community? Are some of them outdated or too vague? Your concerns are important to local representatives. They often gauge what needs to be done by public opinion.

LEGAL

Are local law enforcement agencies enforcing the laws aimed at those who possess or sell drugs? Are parents being notified of suspicious activities that their children may be involved in? The police department is there to protect your rights as a citizen. Part of their responsibilities include making the streets safer for you and your children.

Is it possible for police officers to come into the schools to present prevention talks to students? What about at parent groups? Officers often see a lot more than the average citizen and know pretty much the entire extent of a local drug problem. Are they making this information available to those who are involved in prevention measures?

Are the courts following through with legal consequences? Some deals are often made between the district attorney and the courts. People who are let off the hook rarely learn the lessons that are needed to prevent them from committing the same crimes again. Those involved with drugs need to be punished. Express your concerns with local judges, city attorneys, and prosecuting attorneys.

RELIGIOUS

Churches can play a huge part in getting the message out. Are they sponsoring drug-free activities? If they have adolescent groups, do they know how to identify possible drug problems? Are they aware of how to intervene and assist those who do have a drug problem? Local church leaders are looked up to by many in the community. Getting them involved in prevention efforts is a helpful tool in spreading the message.

Does the church have up-to-date resources available to parents? Are they willing to bring in professionals to speak to parent groups? Can they donate space for drug-free activities? The church can play an important part in bringing people together, kids and adults working on and solving a local drug problem.

PARENT GROUPS

Belonging to a parent group whose primary function is drug prevention among kids is the best way to be involved in prevention efforts. These groups can offer numerous resources as well as support for one another.

They are also a generating factor in getting things done through the approaches that I have outlined above.

If your community does not have a parent group, start one on your own. Get the word out that drugs are a threat to everyone's children and promote the parent group as an effort to keep children off of drugs. Most parents are able and willing to be a part of prevention efforts. Some sit back and wait until someone else makes the first move before they feel comfortable getting involved.

Parent groups are not only instrumental in making needed changes in the community, but are a wealth of help for each individual family. One important task to perform for any parent is to get to know your children's friend's parents. Knowing them can go a long way in making sure your kids don't use or abuse mood or mind altering chemicals. Other parents can be like a second pair of eyes and ears for you. Working together, possible problems can be identified and dealt with before they get out of hand.

Parent groups don't need to be highly organized and structured to be beneficial. Getting together once a week for coffee or tea in individual homes is all that is needed to get a group started. Discussions should center on what the main problems are in the community and on how each parent can do their part to remedy it. A network made up of concerned parents can have a very positive impact in a community.

COMMITMENT

Becoming involved in any or all of these areas takes a lot of commitment on a parent's part. Are you willing to stand by your convictions? At times you may be surprised at the attitudes of some who will try to get in your way to keep you from accomplishing your goals. Try not to be discouraged. If you honestly believe that what you are doing is for the good of your kids and others, then you are a true martyr. The drug problem in this country is strong. It takes an even stronger force to fight it. One key player can make a difference and initiate change. I've seen it happen many times before. As the old saying goes, "Stand up and be counted!"

AFTERWORD

THE DREAM OF A DRUG-FREE WORLD

Picture in your mind waking up one bright sunny morning and sitting down at the breakfast table to read the newspaper. As you scan through it, it dawns on you that there are no printed stories on drugs and crime. There is no news about the degradation of kids brought on by drug abuse. No stories of families torn apart by the claws of addiction. In fact the word "Drug" isn't even mentioned in relation to use, misuse, abuse, or addiction. It's almost as if there weren't a drug problem at all.

As you go about your daily household chores, you turn the television on to keep you company. What you do not hear are tales about teenage suicides, overdoses, or other fatalities. The feeling that something drastically is missing crosses your mind. What is it? What seems to be so different?

The radio is tuned into the number one area station and the hourly news leaves out all the horrors of drug use. There's still national and local news, but nothing that makes a reference to illegal substances. There's no talk about children losing their minds or their lives. This seems to be edited out as if it were some kind of a conspiracy. But, what kind of a conspiracy could it be?

It's late afternoon and the sound of the school bus is heard out front of the house. The door swings open and in walks your child. A smile is firmly planted on the face of this precious one. Arms reach out to hug you and the words, "I love you," are heard. The overwhelming feeling of comfort sweeps through you. The realization that your child is safe makes it's way into your thoughts.

The dream has come true. The world has been rid of all drugs that are a threat to everyone. There's no more fear of having to be confronted with the possibility of a child whose life will be affected by chemicals. All the children in all the world are safe. The search for a drug-free world is over. It's arrival is at your front door. Rest assured now, your child is secure.

Key players have great visions. They hope for the best and set out to see these hopes come true. We may never see a drug-free world in our lifetime. The most we can hope for is a drug-free child. How I have often dreamed of drug-free kids, parents who are willing to put effort into drug prevention, and elimination of the entire threat of drugs.

My dream for you is that you will choose to be a key player on your kid's drug-proofing team. That you will make a winning effort at making that young life healthy and stable. Kids need dedicated players on their team. They need a key player who is willing to give all that they have got to see this dream come true. The stars of the team are your kid and you. Both of you together, not apart. A team works best with solidarity.

I dream that you will follow the principles set down in this book and work toward a drug-free future not only for your child but for all other children. I believe that children deserve the best that they can get out of life. The best can not come with the threat of drugs making an impact on them. We must work to be stronger than this threat. Being a key player on your kid's drug-proofing team is the greatest thing needed to win this game. I urge you to stay on the field and fight. This will be the most important game that you could ever wish to win.

I dream that your kid learns that life can be beautiful without the need for drugs. That the future holds far more possibilities for the drug-free person. And that if drugs are a problem currently in his or her life, that quitting now will set him or her on a path that holds far less problems. A path that will lead into worlds that the child would otherwise have to pass up.

Any child that has a key player on the team has the best chance of growing up drug-free. The foundation built by parents will stand upright for many years to come. I hope that you have the same dreams as I do.

I hope that you have the same thought as I do. That
dreams do come true.

RECOMMENDED READING

Raising Drug-Free Kids in a Drug-Filled World. Perkins, William Mack and Nancy McMurtrie-Perkins. Hazelden Educational Materials. Scranton, PA. 1986.

Not My Kid: A Parent's Guide to Kids and Drugs. Polson, Beth and Miller Newton, Ph.D. Avon. Dresden, TN. 1985.

Growing Up Drug-Free: A Parent's Guide to Prevention. U.S. Department of Education. Diane Publications. Upland, PA. 1993.

Peer Pressure Reversal, An Adult Guide to Developing a Responsible Child. Scott, Sharon. Human Resource Development Press. Amherst, MA. 1985.

Kids and Drugs: A Handbook for Parents and Professionals. Tobias, Joyce. PANDA Press. Annandale, VA. 1989

OTHER RESOURCES

The following agencies and organizations can be helpful in providing you with additional and up-to-date information on the prevention of alcohol and other drug abuse.

Department of Education
Drug Planning and Outreach
Washington, DC   20202
(202) 401-3030

National Institute on Alcohol Abuse and Alcoholism
5600 Fishers Lane, Room 14C-17
Rockville, MD 20857
(301) 443-2954

Office for Substance Abuse Prevention
5600 Fishers Lane
Rockwall II, Room 9A-54
Rockville, MD 20857
(301) 443-0365

Al-Anon Family Groups
P.O. Box 862
Midtown Station
New York, NY 10018
1-800-344-2666

Alcohol and Drug Problems Association of North
    America
1400 I Street, N.W., Suite 1275
Washington, DC 20005
(202) 289-6755

Alcoholics Anonymous
15 E. 26th Street, Room 1810
New York, NY 10010
(212) 683-3900

American Council for Drug Education
204 Monroe Street, Suite 110
Rockville, MD 20850
1-800-488-DRUG

Families Anonymous, Inc.
P.O. Box 528
Van Nuys, CA 91408
(818) 989-7841

Johnson Institute
7151 Metro Boulevard
Minneapolis, MN 55435
1 -800-231 -5165

Mothers Against Drunk Driving
511 E. John Carpenter Freeway, Suite 700
Irving, TX 75062
(214) 744-6233

Narcotics Anonymous
P.O. Box 9999
Van Nuys, CA 91409
(818) 780-3951

National Asian Pacific-American Families Against
Drug Abuse
6303 Friendship Court
Bethesda, MD 20817
(301) 530-0945

National Clearinghouse for Alcohol and Drug
Information
P.O. Box 2345
Rockville, MD 20852
(301) 468-2600

National Council on Alcoholism
12 W. 21st. Street, 7th Floor
New York, NY 10010
(212) 206-6770

National Families in Action
2296 Henderson Mill Road,Suite 204
Atlanta, GA 30345
(404) 934-6364

National Federation of Parents for Drug-free Youth
9551 Big Bend
St. Louis, MO 63122
(314) 968-1322

The National PTA
700 N. Rush Street
Chicago, IL 60611
(312) 787-0977

Parent Resource Institute forDrug Education (PRIDE)
50 Hurt Plaza, Suite 210
Atlanta, GA 30303
(404) 577-4500

INDEX

AUTHOR'S NOTE

Critics are calling this book "The most powerful resource available in the saving of a child's life." If you, your school, employer, or organization has found this book beneficial in guiding kids to be drug-free, I would love to hear from you. If you have suggestions of ways to raise parent awareness of this important resource, please tell me. I truly believe this book can and will make a difference toward the future of a drug-free America.

If you are interested in purchasing "DRUGS and KIDS" in bulk for parents, schools, employers, groups, or organizations or if you want information on workshops, lectures, or consulting, please contact Dick Lutz at the address below:

DRUGS and KIDS
c/o DIMI PRESS
3820 Oak Hollow Lane, SE
Salem, OR 97302-4774
1-503-364-7698
FAX: 1-503-364-9727
E-mail: dickbook@aol.com

MORE ABOUT THE AUTHOR

Gary L. Somdahl is a popular lecturer, therapist, drug prevention consultant, and trainer of parents in how to keep their kids off drugs. His articles on parenting have appeared in many publications. He is a monthly advice columnist for a national teen magazine and has been interviewed on TV and radio shows across the U.S. Also, he has filmed a 13 part series called "Drugs and Kids" for TV.

ORDER FORM

Name _____

Address _____

City/State/Zip _____

Phone _____

Enclosed is my check for $17.95 ($14.95 for *DRUGS and KIDS* and $3 for shipping).

DIMI PRESS
3820 Oak Hollow Lane, SE
Salem, OR 97302-4774

Phone 1-800-644-DIMI(3464) for orders
or 1-503-364-7698 for further information
or FAX to 1-503-364-9727
or by INTERNET to dickbook@aol.com

Call toll-free and order now!

WARNER MEMORIAL LIBRARY
EASTERN COLLEGE
ST. DAVIDS, PA. 19087

OTHER DIMI PRESS PRODUCTS FOR YOU

TAPES are available for...$7.95 each
  #1-LIVE LONGER, RELAX
  #2-ACTIVE RELAXATION
  #3-CONQUER YOUR SHYNESS
  #4-CONQUER YOUR DEPRESSION
  #5-CONQUER YOUR FEARS
  #6-CONQUER YOUR INSOMNIA
  #7-CONQUER YOUR CANCER
  #8-LAST LONGER, ENJOY SEX MORE
  #9-WEIGHT CONTROL
  #10-STOP SMOKING
  #11-LIVE LONGER, RELAX (female voice)
  #12-ACTIVE RELAXATION (female voice)
  #13-UNWIND WHILE DRIVING
  #14-RELAX AWHILE
  #15-RELAX ON THE BEACH/MEADOW
  #16-HOW TO MEDITATE
TAPE ALBUM has six cassettes and is titled:
  GUIDE TO RELAXATION $29.95

BOOKS:

WRESTLING BACK is a true account of an athlete and his mother struggling to recover from his devastating injury.......**$14.95**

BUILD IT RIGHT! is a book of advice on what to watch out for as you build your own home..**$16.95**

FEEL BETTER! LIVE LONGER! RELAX is a manual of relaxation techniques and a history of relaxation............................**$9.95**

HOW TO FIND THOSE HIDDEN JOBS helps job-seekers or career-changers in their search...**$13.95**

BRING ME A MEMORY is a touching story of an 11-yr.-old girl who loses her father **$9.95**

KOMODO, THE LIVING DRAGON (Rev. Ed.) is the only account of the world's largest lizard **$14.95**